What Others are

MW01616461

Those who struggle with the daily challenges of Stage 4 cancer and those who love them will treasure the faithlifting wisdom and practical insights shared in *Stage 4: Your Diagnosis Is Not Your Destiny*. I wish I had this book when I felt helpless and hopeless after what seemed to be a dire diagnosis. If you want to read emotionally real, hope-filled stories of others who faced Stage 4 cancer, I highly recommend this book.

~ Georgia Shaffer, Stage 4 cancer survivor, Professional Certified Coach, PA Licensed Psychologist, and author of *A Gift of Mourning Glories: Restoring Your Life after Loss*

The word *cancer* can strike fear in the heart of anyone. Carole Lewis strikes right back with the hope of God found in Jesus Christ, beautifully written.

~Vicki Heath, National Director, First Place for Health

Stage 4 is a beautifully honest weaving of the author's journey through her husband's cancer experience, her friend Allyson and her husband's accounts of Allyson's Stage 4 years, and others' stories as well. What we are left with at the book's end is a divine tapestry of faith, hope, and love. I highly recommend this book for anyone affected by a Stage 4 diagnosis. I wish I'd had this book when I was caring for my sister during her final hospice months after her Stage 4 diagnosis."

~Janet Holm McHenry, speaker and author of 24 books, including the bestselling *PrayerWalk* and *The Complete Guide to the Prayers of Jesus*

CAROLE LEWIS

Stage 4

YOUR DIAGNOSIS IS *NOT* YOUR DESTINY

Stage 4

Your Diagnosis Is Not
Your Destiny

Carole Lewis

Bold Vision Books
PO Box 2011
Friendswood, Texas 77549

Dedication

I am dedicating this book to my friend, Joy Stephens and her son, John.

When I was a young mom, Joy was my first mentor in the faith. She gave me my first journal in 1972 and inscribed it with "For Your First Book."

John has become very precious to me because of his life and love for his wife, Allyson, whose story is shared throughout this book. John has become the man he is today in large part, because of his and Allyson's 25-year journey with Stage 4.

Table of Contents

Acknowledgments

All of us are who we are today, whether good or bad, because of what was sowed into our lives by others. I am grateful for every person who has sowed the love of Christ into my life.

My parents accepted Christ at the ages of 34 and 38 when I was 5 years old, and my life was forever shaped by this event. I also want to acknowledge the influence of mentors like Marge Caldwell, Zig Ziglar, and Florence Littauer.

Marge showed me how to laugh during trials. Zig taught me the value of positive living, and Florence inspired me to tell my story with excellence, whether in speaking or writing.

I have had mentors all along the way in my life and I remember each one's contribution. May I spend the rest of my life not only acknowledging those who have taught me but being that kind of person in the lives of others.

Introduction

The number 4 has great significance. In biblical numerology, the number 4 is the number of completion. God created the material earth on the 4th day. He created the earth with 4 sides: north, south, east, and west. There are 4 elements in creation: earth, air, fire, and water. Every year has 4 seasons—summer, autumn, winter, and spring. The moon has four phases.

There are many Stage-4 times in life, too. In football, there are the 4th down and the 4th quarter. All the 4s indicate that something is ending. It isn't over, but we're seeing the end in sight.

A Stage 4 cancer diagnosis is jarring and life changing because in the beginning we see it as a sentence of death. As you read the stories of living a long time with Stage 4 cancer, my prayer is that you will be filled with hope and determine to not give in or give up. God loves you and will hold your hand every step of the way. This book will tell the stories of six people who have lived from thirteen to over thirty years with Stage 4 cancer. May you be encouraged and find hope on those days you need it most.

1

The Unwanted Gift

A woman in my Bible study class spoke to me right before I was to teach. She said she had cancer which had spread to various organs. She asked for some verses to help her. As we talked, a big tear rolled down both my cheeks because I flashed back to the terror and fear of the dreaded diagnosis of Stage 4.

If you are holding this book, you have heard the dreaded words Stage 4. Maybe you heard the word at your last doctor's appointment, or you have a friend or loved one who has heard the words. You want hope and you want to know how to give hope. The first thing I want you to do is stop. Take some deep breaths. Breathe in hope, and breathe out fear.

This book will primarily address Stage 4 cancer, but every major disease has four Stages. And by the time the disease reaches Stage 4, it is serious. If you think about it, we are all at Stage 4. I was shocked when I heard my pastor preaching about leaving a legacy. He waved his hand across our giant congregation and said, "In 100 years, none of you sitting in this sanctuary will be alive."

Some, like me, are in Stage 4 of life because of our age. This year I celebrated my 79th birthday and even though my health is still excellent, I thought about how many years I might have left. My mom died at 89, so this year the thought hit me. *I might only have ten years left if I live as long as my mom.* Sobering.

Others are in Stage 4 of their marriage and may not even know it. They have neglected to nurture their marriage, and both have grown apart for whatever reason. The marriage is in precarious shape because of neglect and ripe for affairs and divorce.

There are many who are in Stage 4 with their finances. They have maxed out their credit cards, have no money in savings, and are at risk of losing their home because they don't have the money to make the payment. The catalyst that brings Stage 4 to a head is usually the loss of the job that has helped them keep up the façade.

More than we care to think about are in Stage 4 just because they have neglected taking care of their body.

High blood pressure, diabetes, heart disease, and obesity put them at great risk of the lingering malaise of poor health or sudden death.

Even though Stage 4 is an unwanted gift, it has the power to change you and me in ways that are beautiful to behold as God changes us from the inside and out. It is never too late to make life-giving changes in any area of Stage 4.

The goal of this book is to help you see that a diagnosis of Stage 4 is only a diagnosis and not a destination. In the beginning, it seems like a death sentence because of the fear of the unknown avenger inside the body. Although this diagnosis is terrifying and unwanted, you will get past the diagnosis and learn how to live again. Stage 4 cannot be cured but take heart. You and I have a God who determines how long each of us will live. A verse in the Bible says, "Your eyes saw my unformed body. All the days ordained for me were written in Your book before one of them came to be" (Psalm 139:16). None of us are going anywhere until God calls us home, and my prayer for you is that you get your hope renewed and that you will fight the avenger with everything in you. You can live a long time with Stage 4, so don't give up.

When the doctors diagnosed my husband Johnny with Stage 4 prostate cancer, he was 58 years old. He lived almost seventeen years after being given the grim prognosis of only two years to live. Johnny and I walked every step of this journey together and learned so many amazing truths along the way. Prior to the Stage 4 diagnosis, we lived life as though we would both live a long life and die just days apart at the ripe old age of 99. I realized years into the journey that most of us live life like this. We take life for granted and fail to realize how precious each day is on this earth. We live as if we have forever to make a difference in our world, and life keeps rolling along until we hear the dreaded words, "I'm sorry to have to tell you that you have Stage 4 cancer."

I have written fifteen books, but for some crazy reason I never wanted to write about our cancer journey. I guess I felt the subject was too heavy and that people with Stage 4 cancer wouldn't want to hear about our story. The last six months have drastically changed my perspective because I have been drawn into another family's journey and realize that Stage 4 cancer can change everything and many times, change it for the better.

I met Allyson Bell more than 30 years ago. She was a young woman in her early twenties who had graduated from nursing school with plans to become an oncology nurse. Allyson grew up in Dyer, Tennessee, and was dating John Paul. He was the son of my dear friends, Paul and Joy Stephens, who lived in Austin, Texas, where Paul was pastoring and Joy was teaching first grade. I had worked for ten years as Paul's secretary when he pastored a church in Houston. His wife Joy was, and still is, one of my mentors and best friends in this world. John Paul seemed like one of our kids and spent many happy times with our family when his parents traveled. My husband, Johnny, coached John Paul in football, so we have a strong family connection.

While I was visiting Paul and Joy, Allyson was in Austin visiting John Paul. John was at work, so Allyson spent the day with us. We drove to Fredericksburg to shop. She and I had a delightful day visiting in the back seat of the car. I fell in love with her and told John if he didn't marry Allyson, he was a fool.

John and Allyson were married and had two sons, Tyler and Ben. Then at age 28, Allyson was diagnosed with Stage 1 breast cancer. Tyler was 3, and Ben was 6 months old. We were full of hope that she might be cured since it was in the early Stage, but two years later the cancer came back with a vengeance at Stage 4. While Allyson was given six months to live, she lived another 23 years despite her dire prognosis.

John's Thoughts on Receiving the Unwanted Gift of a Stage 4 Cancer

I am sure whoever is holding this book is looking for hope and encouragement. Hurting or worried about a recent diagnosis or knows someone who is hurting that needs encouragement. This book will give you encouragement and allow you to walk with confidence, regardless of the circumstances. Allyson lived with Stage 4 cancer for many years and found a peace that surpassed all understanding. She loved reading the Psalms and felt a connection with David. She fully understood him because he was a man after God's own heart, yet he would voice his frustration at the same time. Allyson felt the same way. Seeking God and praising him for his goodness and watchful, caring eyes as he orchestrated each situation. He was in control. However, Allyson was discouraged many times in her journey, and she would not hold back her frustration and disappointment in the circumstances. She was outspoken, especially with me ... "What did I do to deserve this?" "Why is God mad at me?" "I had the perfect life and somehow cancer wants to destroy me?" "He is in control but yet He allows this illness to remain?" I learned how to listen. At first, I told her how much God loved her, I was praying for her, God is good, etc. ... but over a period of time, I realized she wasn't seeking a response from me, she just wanted to voice her frustration and be heard. It was healthy for her to vent, and listening to her intently was what she needed from me. And all the way thru the cancer visits and multiple diagnosis, I realized she needed to know I understood her. She and I both recognized our faith journey was enhancing our relationship, and our lives were enriched with each doctor's visit. Each day together was another blessed day. When facing the unknown, our priorities changed. We invested more time in our kids. We sought others who were hurting to give them encouragement. We slowed down and treasured each moment together as a blessing from above.

One day, I approached Allyson with a question. I needed to hear her answer because I realized my thinking had changed. "If God were to allow a do-over and we could erase the past and start anew going back to the first doctor visit, would you choose a different path?" Her answer was the same as mine. "No, I have so much to be thankful for. My faith is stronger. My life is sweeter. My love is deeper. My eyes have been opened." At some point we both transitioned from fear and discouragement to courage and strength. Walking by faith is a blessed walk. It's treacherous but our lives were enriched as each day was lived with a greater purpose. Hard to imagine that something like cancer can make life so much more meaningful, but God's Word has a way of changing you when faced with the unknown.

Throughout the book I will share our story first, followed by John and Allyson's story. Although I only have first-hand knowledge of Johnny and Allyson, I know many others who have lived years with Stage 4 cancer, so take heart and keep breathing deep. Allyson was a blogger, so I will also share one of her blogs at the end of each chapter.

I want you to have an active part in the transformation God wants to do in you, so I will ask you to take three steps as each chapter ends.

1. pray with me.
2. journal your thoughts
3. memorize a verse of Scripture

These steps will reprogram your heart and mind with hope.

I will also share some stories in this book of dear friends who have lived many years with Stage 4 cancer. The first is my friend, Georgia Shaffer, who has lived with Stage 4 since 1989. I am sharing Georgia's story first because she has lived the longest and is as radiant and vibrant today as when I first met her 20 years ago.

Georgia Shaffer

Georgia Shaffer knows what it's like to face a frightening future after the diagnosis of Stage 4 breast cancer and later lung, ovarian, and colon cancer. She also understands what it takes to rebuild after unwanted changes and create a hope-filled future. Georgia is a professional certified coach (PCC) who offers one-on-one and group coaching for women. One of her groups, ReBUILD, is for those who are divorced and struggling to begin again after a shattered marriage. As a licensed psychologist in Pennsylvania, she is also the author of five books, including *A Gift of Mourning Glories: Restoring Your Life after Loss, Taking Out Your Emotional Trash* and *Avoiding the 12 Relationship Mistakes Women Make*. Georgia is a recipient of the American Association of Christian Counselors (AACC) Award for Excellence in Christian Caregiving. For free resources visit www.GeorgiaShaffer.com.

Georgia Shaffer (email Georgia@GeorgiaShaffer.com)

The Power of One

It was one of those moments you never forget. For me, it was a chilly day in January. I sat in the examining room, waiting for the results of yet another biopsy. Six months earlier, at the age of 38, I had been diagnosed with breast cancer and had a mastectomy and reconstruction. But then a rash had appeared on my reconstructed breast, and now I waited for the results of that biopsy.

The verdict? Recurrence of breast cancer.

My reaction? I was devastated.

It was nothing like the first time I was told I had cancer. There was no insulating shock. There was no numbness of disbelief. This time, there was no denying what was happening. It was serious, and I knew it. Fear was the only emotion I felt.

Although I can't recall what my doctor said that day, I remember what happened when he left the room. Vicki, his assistant, was only a few years younger than I, and she stood there looking very troubled about my situation. I took one glance at her and burst into tears. "I don't want to die. My son is only nine years old. I want to live to see him graduate from high school."

I cried, and I cried, and I kept repeating, "I just want to live to see my son graduate from high school."

Vicki didn't tell me I would see my son graduate. She didn't tell me I wouldn't. She listened, held me tightly, and handed me one tissue after another. I don't know how long I was there, but I know she ached with me. There have been so many times since then that I've reflected on that event. And always that devastating moment is softened by the memory of Vicki's tenderness and compassion. It made all the difference.

Obviously, that wasn't the end of my story. I went back to my oncologist only to be told I had a 2 percent chance of being alive in ten years. My only hope for long-term survival was chemotherapy, radiation, and a bone marrow transplant. He said, "Georgia, there is a fine line between killing you or killing the cancer."

He was right. I had all those treatments and when they were complete, I was in remission. But as my son said years later, "Mom, you were a ghost in a shell."

I learned through that experience. I learned life is fragile. Even though we often think we understand we will die someday, it wasn't until I was given a terminal diagnosis, the harsh reality registered in my heart. I became intentional to live and make whatever time I had count.

I also learned that one person, like Vicki, can make a powerful and positive impact in the life of another. No matter how brief the interaction, empathy is truly a gift.

After my bone marrow transplant, I had a fever of 104 degrees for a week and grew weaker and weaker physically. But the lack of physical energy was replaced by a spiritual strength. I experienced the Lord's comfort and peace in a way I never had before. It was that spiritual closeness, unconditional love, and taste of heaven that changed my life forever.

After the transplant, I spent most of my days in bed. I could not do simple things like the laundry or go to the grocery store. When Kyle, my son, was home from school, he often put a frying pan on my bed with a wooden stick and said, "Mom,

I am going downstairs to play Nintendo. If you need me, just hit the frying pan with the stick and I'll be right up."

Kyle had watched me go from an energetic get-it-done mom attending grad school and working at Penn State York as a manager and instructor to someone who often mustered all her strength just to sit up in bed or in a chair when he came home from grade school.

As a mom, I did not want to die, but I honestly wasn't afraid to die because I now had a deep connection with Jesus. In many ways, it would have been a relief to die because I did not know how I could ever move beyond the difficult place I was in. To add to my physical challenges, during this same period, I also went through a divorce and lost my job because I was too weak to work. So many days I buried my head in my hands and sobbed, "God, I can't do this. It's too hard."

I learned, or was forced, to rely on God like I never had before. There is nothing–I mean nothing–like brokenness or pain to provide the right conditions for spiritual growth. I felt like the Apostle Paul when he wrote,

"We were under great pressure, far beyond our ability to endure, so that we despaired of life itself. Indeed, we felt we had received the sentence of death. But this happened that we might not rely on ourselves but on God" (2 Corinthians.1:8,9 NIV).

From experience, I can tell you God can transform the most hopeless of situations, but he usually does so one step at a time. With each step he gives us the opportunity to know him better and to love him more completely.

Twenty-three years passed. I was now an author, a speaker, and a professional certified coach when I was diagnosed with Stage 4 lung cancer and given one year to live.

This time there was no longer the fear of Kyle growing up without a mom. I had seen him graduate from college and danced with him at his wedding. He knew the Lord and had experienced for himself the difference a relationship with God makes.

As a result of this most recent diagnosis (given six years ago), I became even more passionate and intentional about helping others rebuild after unwanted change. I want to reignite the dying spark in people who look at their future and cannot see things ever getting better. Whether someone is separated or divorced, living with a chronic illness like cancer or MS, or experiencing a major change they never would have chosen, I want to support and encourage them as they grieve. I want to guide them to that day when they can begin anew. If I can help them avoid some of the common mistakes that keep people stuck in their intense sadness, anger, or resentment, I will have fulfilled my calling.

For me, it isn't about how long I live. It's about what kind of difference I can make with the life God grants me. Like Vicki on that cold winter day so long ago, I pray that with the help and strength of Jesus, I am making a positive difference in the lives of those I love, work with, or meet.

Pray With Me

Dear Lord, You are the God of hope. I am asking You to wrap Your arms of love around us as we read this book. Fill us with joy and peace as we trust in You so that our lives will overflow with hope by the power of Your Holy Spirit. In Jesus' name, amen.

Journal

Write about where you are right now. You will want to look back at where you were at the beginning of this journey in years to come. You can freely pour out your heart to God with whatever emotions you are experiencing. God can handle your fear, anger, or doubt that He can or will help you. He wants to help you and will walk every step of this journey with you. Ask Him to do that.

Verse To Memorize

"May the God of hope fill you with all joy
and peace as you trust in Him, so that you
may overflow with hope by the power of
the Holy Spirit" (Romans 15:13).

Allyson's Blog
A Walk in the Fog

One morning this week, the fog was so thick that when I got back from my walk, it seemed I had just stepped out of the shower. Fog. While it is intriguing, it also obscures and gives false illusions about reality.

I have been thinking about an incident that happened when all I could see in front of me was the heaviness of the circumstance—dark, thick, nasty fog. I was driving from one office to the next during my lunch break and was the first one on the scene of a horrific accident involving a car and a semi. The driver of the car suffered a laceration to his jugular vein. There was nothing I could do except apply pressure and wait for the paramedics.

After a few minutes, his vitals plummeted, and I knew his life was slipping away. I could hear the paramedics say as I walked to my car, "we are losing him." Being a nurse, I had seen people die before, but this was different and more disturbing. The next day, I called the local ER and was told he had expired in transit. For the next few weeks, I grieved a stranger's death.

Fast forward to a day when I was not quite 31 years old and woke up in a recovery room from a double mastectomy. I will never forget the sound next to me of my mother weeping. I wasn't fully awake from the anesthesia, but in my spirit, I asked God why He didn't love me anymore. It's what I felt. He knows our hearts. So why not just say it out loud, "Why had He forsaken me?" What I heard was silence, but what I saw was a man standing over me explaining why I needed to breathe into a mask. I noticed a large scar on his neck, and he seemed vaguely familiar. I asked him what had happened, and he told me how he had died six times after a tragic accident and spent six months in the hospital.

Very few moments come full circle in my life, but in that instant, it did. It wasn't by coincidence that the ER had given me the wrong information, or that for the past four years, we had worked in the same medical building and never crossed paths. I knew one reason God had saved him was for this moment—to fill me with hope and to remind me that He is always at work in my circumstances. The gift of our reunion that day wasn't only for me, but for him as well. He was so overcome with emotion, he had to leave my room to compose himself.

Like me, his life was on a downward spiral. He was questioning God's presence. His marriage had crumbled, and he was struggling with alcoholism. He knew it was not by accident that I was his patient that day. His hope had been renewed, and he felt tremendous gratitude to help me in my time of need.

The scientific reason we can't see through the fog is because billions of water particles scatter the light. When I am in a season of life that feels more than overwhelming, the truths of God are distorted and scattered. It is at those times that I ask God to open the eyes of my heart rather than the eyes in my head, and to help me quietly trust Him.

~Allyson

2

The Dreaded Diagnosis

In June we had taken a group to Israel and Johnny complained of groin pain when we did steep climbs. After we returned, he self-diagnosed that it was the return of a hernia removed twelve years before, so we set up an appointment with the surgeon to get it checked out. The surgeon examined Johnny and said, "This is no hernia; you need to see a urologist." A series of biopsies and scans led to the news of Stage 4 prostate cancer, which had spread to his bones.

One month before Johnny's diagnosis, we purchased a little home on Galveston Bay. While I traveled that summer, Johnny searched for a perfect second home for us to purchase. We finally found a house right on the waterfront that had a rental clientele. I was happy because we could rent it out and just spend a couple of weeks a year in it—or so I thought.

Three days before his diagnosis, our son's home burned to the ground. And John, his wife Lisa, and their three children moved into our home in Houston with only the clothes on their backs. Everything was gone. The day Johnny had all his scans, we told the kids we were going to drive to our little bay house after we finished, sensing that the news might not be good.

We never came back home. John and his family lived in our home in Houston for almost two years while they built a new home on their original homesite. They had lived about a mile from us, so their kids caught the same bus to school each day and kept their same friends the entire time. They had absolutely everything they needed, living in our fully furnished home.

I'll never forget the day of Johnny's diagnosis. I dropped him off early at the hospital for a full day of scans. If I had known what we would face at the end of that day, I wouldn't have left Johnny's side for a minute. I was clueless, so I went about my day in the usual way, including lunch with a woman we were considering hiring. During lunch I found out that the woman was a recent widow, and I asked her what her husband died from, and she said, "prostate cancer." When I asked how long he lived after diagnosis she said, "Three months." I became increasingly anxious during the afternoon.

When I picked Johnny up at the hospital, our former internist, now the head of the nuclear medicine department at the hospital, invited me into his office. He told me that Johnny was having another bone scan because they wanted to confirm what they saw on the first scan. He looked at me and with the saddest eyes said, "I hate to tell you this, but Johnny has prostate cancer that has spread to his bones. Seven of the eight biopsied sites are malignant, so this means his cancer is Stage 4." Johnny walked into his office and heard the news, too. I sobbed quietly while the two of them talked about the diagnosis. The doctor said our only option was to begin hormone therapy.

I was a wreck. Johnny hadn't eaten a bite the entire day and wanted to stop at a Mexican restaurant on the way to the bay. It was October and already dark at 6 pm when we arrived at the restaurant. I had been crying the entire ride and didn't think I could go inside. Johnny said, "Put on my sunglasses and no one will know." We sat down in a corner with me facing the wall and ordered dinner. My shoulders kept heaving, so I'm sure the other customers thought Johnny was a wife beater. True to form, I could eat all my dinner because I've always believed if I eat something, I'll feel better.

At the bay, I couldn't stop crying and finally said, "I'm so sorry I can't be strong for you," to which he replied, "How do you think I would feel if you were strong right now?" We both laughed and crawled up in the middle of the bed and prayed together. I immediately calmed down and allowed God to comfort my broken heart. We never went back to our home in Houston to live. Our kids settled into our Houston home, and we settled into life at the bay, living in that little house for the next two years.

❧

I wasn't there when John and Allyson heard her dreaded diagnosis, so I asked John to give me his account of their story.

I was at work when I got the first phone call. She asked me to come to the office because her doctor wanted to visit with both of us. I pressed her as to why I had to leave work early to hear what the doctor could tell her. She said she had cancer, and he wanted to discuss treatment plans. It was a long forty-five-minute drive. That first diagnosis was treated as a non-event. A lumpectomy and radiation, with a small chance of it ever returning again.

Two years later (Ben was 2 ½ years old and Tyler was 5 ½ years old), we received word that the tests showed the cancer had metastasized and was in her lymph nodes. Dr Cagle was emotional when he told Allyson there was not an effective treatment plan and her prognosis was not good, with little hope of surviving another 6 months. Dr Cagle, her oncologist, loved Allyson as she had worked for him. He spent countless hours researching her case, and I remember him taking off his glasses and reluctantly told her to quit her job, take the kids out of day care, and spend every hour with them. When we got home, Allyson buried her head in my chest and said that she had asked God to let her live long enough that her boys would remember her. She wanted the boys to know that she loved them more than anything, and she always wanted to be a loving mother and all that she had dreamed of was being taken away. She asked that I pray with her, requesting that God would answer her prayer and allow her to live long enough to experience being a "mom."

We started treatments shortly thereafter, but the prognosis was still six months. It didn't matter if she took chemo or not it was still a six-month lifespan. Allyson was about two treatments into a round of 16 or so chemo sessions when she developed pneumonia. We rushed her to the hospital. She was close to death, and the doctors had to wash out the chemo for her to have enough white cells to fight off the virus and bacteria. She barely made it thru that scare.

After she was released from the hospital, she started over with chemo treatments. About halfway through the round, we both woke up at three in the morning. We were wide awake, and Allyson said she felt led to pray. I prayed with her for hours. When we finished praying, Allyson said she felt a warmth in her that was not natural. She felt as if she was healed of this disease, and her countenance changed from that point on. She was upbeat and no longer tearful. She spoke at churches about her ordeal and how she believed that God was moving in her life and would grant her long life despite the diagnosis. It was after her chemo treatment that we followed Johnny and Carole with a fasting regimen they were doing since Johnny had just been diagnosed with Stage 4 prostate cancer. Allyson started working out regularly, and her energy was back, and her outlook was positive. I believe she went 5 years with no reoccurrence and life was good.

❧

Each person has their own *dreaded diagnosis* story. If you are that person who has Stage 4 cancer, I'm sure you remember the time and day vividly. When you received the news, your first thought was that you had received a death sentence. God allows us time to grieve those awful moments as long as we need to, but there will come a time when something brings a glimmer of hope back into your life. None of us can live without hope, and our God is the God of hope. There is a verse that I memorized years ago that has carried me through the tough times and never failed to fill me with hope.

Pray With Me

Dear Lord, We have received news that has the power to cause us to despair. Help us believe that we will see Your goodness today in the land of the living. In Jesus' name, amen.

Journal

Write about your dreaded diagnosis. Include everything you can remember about that day or days. Your symptoms, or lack of, the discovery of a problem, the tests, and the diagnosis. Write about your feelings and all the emotions you experienced or are still experiencing. How has the diagnosis affected your family and friends?

Verse To Memorize

"I would have despaired if I had not
believed I would see the goodness of the
Lord in the land of the living"
(Psalm 27:13).

Allyson's Blog
Nurturing Hope

I read a line in my devotional that said we need to make sure we are "nurturing our hope." I love the word *nurture* because it stirs up such warm and fuzzy emotions. The word actually means to "encourage the growth and development of." Hope has had incredible power in my life. When standing at my dad's graveside, hope was the only thing that gave my weak legs the strength to walk away, knowing death is not the end.

When faced daily with a chronic illness, hope reminds me that God has the final say. When the world news is overwhelming, hope reminds me earth is not my real home and God has never left His throne. These thoughts are not just my opinions, but truths spoken by God in His Word. Hope may have different meanings for different people, but in my life, it is defined as a verb. An action word implying that I am choosing to fully trust God and the mysteriousness of His ways. It is not by any means a cakewalk for me, but a daily intentional act on my part to trust.

The book of Lamentations is usually not a first pick for a morning read because of its great sorrow expressed by the writer, but along with the lamenting you will find the writer's effort to remain hopeful. In Lamentations 3:21-23 the writer says, "Yet this I call to mind and therefore I hope: Because of the Lord's great love we are not consumed, for His compassions never fail, they are new every morning; great is your faithfulness."

The *whys* and *what ifs* still come, but rather than nurturing these questions, I try to take all negative thoughts captive and make them obedient to Christ. (2 Corinthians 10:5) Please don't miss that I said "try." What does my trying actually look like? When my mind goes to a dark place because it has been nurturing fears of all kinds, I read the Bible and allow His Word to replace my fears with His truth and this nurtures my trust in Him and hope swells up in my soul. It happens every time.

Right behind that hope is the peace and strength that makes little sense to face whatever circumstance He allows. ("And the peace of God, which transcends all understanding, will guard your hearts and minds in Christ Jesus" Philippians 4:7.) Daily, I try to look for ways to encourage the continued growth and development of my hope. Without it I feel lost, confused, and discouraged. Sometimes this means meditating on a truth from His Word, reflecting on His faithfulness during difficult days, taking in the wonder of His creation through nature, or turning up the praise music and simply singing. Hope gives us the power to endure, and Christ never intended for us to live a moment without it.

~Allyson

3

Choosing a Treatment Plan

Most of us after a Stage 4 cancer diagnosis do a lot of research and give a great amount of thought about what treatment plan to choose. We were no different from most. I had been the director of an international wellness program called First Place for Health for ten years at the time of Johnny's diagnosis. A Stage 4 diagnosis is usually a bleak one, so with Johnny's blessing and encouragement, I began looking to see if there was anything holistic we might do instead of hormone therapy, which was only going to work for about two years.

I found a Christian program in Colorado Springs called Health Quarters, which consisted of coffee enemas, juicing, and a vegan diet. I knew that if I didn't do it with Johnny, he would never continue on his own, so we took off for Colorado Springs and spent 11 days learning this regimen. After returning home, we continued on this plan for six months. At the time of diagnosis, Johnny's PSA was 48 and after six months of this strict regimen his PSA was 65. One morning, Johnny said, "This is not living and I'm going to stop doing this." And he did.

We were hopeful this was our miracle, so we shared the plan with John and Allyson after her cancer had returned as Stage 4, and Allyson did the regimen for a time as well.

All of us have to find our way through the maze of treatment options. Do your homework, and God will lead you to the plan that is right for you. I became an expert on prostate cancer, and I don't even have a prostate gland. I studied everything I could find about prostate cancer and most times when our doctor had a prospective patient call Johnny to ask about his treatment, Johnny would talk a minute and say, "My wife, Carole, can help you more than I can. Let me give you to her."

After our six-month coffee enema, juicing, and vegan plan, Johnny decided he wanted to go ahead with hormone therapy. He began treatment with our urologist in Houston, and I began the forty-six-mile drive into Houston to work five days a week. We went on with our lives and the next October I took a week of vacation.

During that week, God revealed to me I had been gone emotionally for the last year. I was astounded because I had worked, traveled, spoken publicly, and felt like I was doing okay. When I returned to work, I shared with my staff what the Lord had revealed to me, and they looked at me like *DUH!* Not only had God been carrying me for the last year, but my staff had also been carrying me.

Not too long after Johnny's diagnosis, we received a VHS tape from a friend in California. Her husband had prostate cancer, and they wanted us to check out their doctor, an oncologist who only treated men with prostate cancer. Men came to Dr Bob Leibowitz from all over the world, so we went to Los Angeles for a consultation. By this time, we had already completed thirteen months of hormone therapy, which followed our six-month trek into the holistic approach, so we were nineteen months out from our initial diagnosis. We took all of Johnny's scans, and I'll never forget what Dr. Bob said to Johnny that day. "Johnny, I can't promise that I can save your life, but I will promise that I can extend it beyond two years (the prognosis we were given 19 months before). That day he became our doctor, and he worked with an oncologist in Houston who followed his instructions for Johnny's care. A year after we moved our primary care to L.A. we found a new publisher for our First Place for Health materials in Ventura, California, just an hour north of L.A. Our God knows everything about us and cares about every detail of our lives. The Gregg family, who owned the publishing house Gospel Light, had an apartment attached to their home for their authors who came to Ventura for meetings. Every time we went to our doctor in L.A., we could stay in the apartment. I went to meetings while Johnny sat outside in a coffee shop, reading in the gorgeous, year-round 72-degree weather of Ventura, California.

It might seem crazy to some that we traveled to L.A. for care when we lived in Houston, Texas, where the leading cancer center in the world is located. One of my favorite sayings is "But God." God had a different plan for Johnny and me, and He provided the perfect doctor and the perfect place to recover after treatment. Originally, after diagnosis, we had gone to the leading cancer center for a second opinion and were told that the only treatment they could offer us was continuous hormone therapy that would only work for approximately two years. After that, the male body becomes resistant to the female hormones and then we might get into a clinical trial. Our oncologist in L.A. did not believe in continuous hormone therapy and told us that every man with Stage 4 prostate cancer should be under the care of an oncologist, not a urologist. Johnny had chemo five times over the course of his disease and had a very good quality of life until the last six months. We always went to L.A. for his first chemo treatment and then our oncologist in Houston administered the rest of the treatments.

Because our doctor in L.A. only treated prostate cancer, he was on the cutting edge of research for the disease. Johnny took several medications a few years before they were approved by the Federal Drug Administration (FDA), and we were always trying something that just might work. Frozen shark cartilage was one of those medicines. After about six months, our doctor said, "Quit doing this; it doesn't work." He had enough patients that he knew pretty quick what worked and what didn't. We stayed with our oncologist in L.A. and our oncologist in Houston for fifteen years and loved them both very much.

❧

Allyson was an oncology nurse and working for an on- cologist at the time of her second diagnosis of Stage 4 cancer. Where we knew nothing about prostate cancer, Allyson knew too much. She perfectly understood her diagnosis and treatment plan.

John and Allyson moved sixty miles from Conroe, Texas, where they lived, to Katy, Texas. Now that her cancer was Stage 4, they prayed about a fresh start and a new beginning. They also believed that some of the best doctors in the world were in Houston. The best part was that now John was five miles from work instead of fifty-five miles. He could go to doctor appointments with Allyson. Because God is in everything, they found the Katy Independent School District to be perfect for their young family. They also found a great local church where they taught and stayed for twenty-five years. God led her to a new doctor, who was also on the cutting edge of oncology, and Allyson stayed under her care for the next twenty years.

God is the only one who has the power to add years to our Stage 4 cancer diagnosis. There is no magic diet or miracle working doctor to be found. God will lead you to the perfect plan for you; your job is to ask Him for wisdom to find that perfect plan. Don't get caught up in the comparison trap, comparing your journey to someone else's. I live my life by this simple phrase, "Do the next right thing." What is the next right thing for you to do today? Do it and tomorrow God will show you what the next right thing is, too.

Stage 4 cancer is a serious, chronic, health condition, but remember, you are going nowhere until the Lord Jesus calls you home. Life is uncertain and that day could be today for many who don't have Stage 4 cancer. None of us knows how much time we have left on this earth, but we can ask God to teach us the same valuable truths that Stage 4 cancer survivors learn on their journey.

Pray With Me

Dear Lord, I pray you will lead us to the perfect treatment plan and that we will know in our heart that this is Your will for our life. Encourage our heart with the truth that You will continue leading us every minute of every day if we will just ask. In Jesus' name, amen.

Journal

Write about the steps you went through to choose a treatment plan. How did God lead you? Was it through a doctor, friend, or loved one? What is your treatment plan? How long will it take?

Verse To Memorize

"Whether you turn to the right or to the left, your ears will hear a voice behind you, saying, 'This is the way; walk in it'" (Isaiah 30:21).

I was living my idea of the perfect life. I had (and still have) a great husband, two super cute little boys, one three-year-old and the other only five months—and a great part-time job allowing me to be at home a lot and yet still have the career I had always wanted. Life was good by my evaluation.

One afternoon in my perfect little world, my dad called to say my mom had breast cancer. She would have surgery immediately, along with a hard round of chemotherapy and radiation to follow. I've always been close to both of my parents, and I felt as if my world had been flipped upside down and my perfectly arranged pieces spilled out. The possibility of losing my mom so soon gripped me with such an intense fear that after we hung up the phone, I sat still and numb. There are many events in my life that I can no longer recall but those that shook me to my core remain crystal clear. This would be the first test of my faith that little did I know would pale compared to the ones to come later.

I recently heard a sermon where the pastor challenged us

as we are entering a new year to ask ourselves, what is the next right thing I am to do?

I remember distinctly asking this same question of God after receiving the news about mom. After getting off the phone with dad I went outside to be alone. For some reason, being outdoors seems to unclog my mind. As I sat in silence before God, I asked a very similar question...

What am I to do next that pleases you and helps me to move forward?

At first, I heard nothing but the sounds in my head—fear, anger, and it's not fair. Years of being churched and studying the Bible, and not one verse would come to mind. This led to a frustrated determination to continue to sit, pray, and ask God to remind me of a verse, anything that would calm my anxious thoughts. After more than an hour, I must have finally stilled and humbled myself before Him and I heard it.

"Rejoice always, pray continually, give thanks in all circumstances, for this is God's will for you in Christ Jesus" (1 Thessalonians 5:16-18).

It was clear direction, but not the message I had in mind that God would give me, so I dismissed it and waited for another. Isn't that just how we are sometimes? God quietly speaks into our circumstance telling us how to move forward, but when we don't like the message, we just sit and wait for another.

I can't help but wonder as I think back on times I prayed for clarity with situations if maybe sometimes, the problem was with me not utilizing the clarity He had already provided. There are more than a few times I can instantly think of where God gave me the direction I needed and then waited and waited and waited some more for me to follow it.

All along, I am usually seeking a path that I like, one that is easy, and one that makes sense to me. Isaiah 55:8 clearly reminds us that God's ways are not our ways, and His thoughts are not our thoughts yet many times we expect every directive He gives us to make sense in the moment—or at least I do.

The next right thing for me to do was to rejoice, pray, and be thankful. I heard no other message that day.

~Allyson

4

Priorities Change

A radical shift in priorities happens after a Stage 4 diagnosis. Once important concerns are no longer important. The unimportant now takes on greater significance. A big priority in my life was my job with First Place for Health. I still loved my job, but after our Stage 4 diagnosis, Johnny now became my main priority. Before the diagnosis, I might stay after work to attend a women's Bible study, but now I came right home after work to spend time with him. Meetings and fun times with friends no longer had a place of importance in my life.

Realizing that you may not have forever to do what you thought you had forever to do changes all your priorities. As I look back over our Stage 4 cancer journey, I see how God worked on our behalf and changed our outlook.

We live in a fallen world where bad happens to us and all around us. Jesus brings us to the other side of those grim experiences better and stronger than we ever thought possible. God orchestrated circumstance after circumstance to change our priorities, which led to His perfect will for us.

Johnny died June 27, 2014, just one day after our 55th wedding anniversary. I had retired in January after twenty seven years as director of First Place for Health. I retired because I knew the time had come that Johnny needed me full time by his side. He'd lived more than sixteen years with Stage 4 prostate cancer. He'd had a very good quality of life until he began having bone pain because the treatments were no longer working, and his cancer markers were skyrocketing. Johnny died one month before his 75th birthday and never lost his delightful sense of humor. A few weeks before he died, he asked, "Am I going to be 75 on my birthday?" When I said, "Yes" he replied, "Well that would be old if I didn't have cancer." Johnny lived with Stage 4 cancer almost seventeen years, and I never once heard him complain or ask, "Why me?"

After his diagnosis, our good marriage became a great marriage. We never wasted another day by neglecting to say, "I love you." We kissed in the morning and at night and no longer sweated the small stuff, because everything after this kind of diagnosis is small stuff. I think about Johnny every time I walk into a hotel room because when he was alive and I had to travel, the first thing I did when I walked into a hotel room was call him to let him know I got there safely and to see how he was doing.

God was working when we bought a second home at the bay. It was kind of like when your husband wants to buy a new car; he trashes the car you have, saying it's not worth repairing. I learned long ago that if it's going to happen, just accept it. This is exactly the way I felt about buying a second home; it was going to happen. My prayer was that it would be one we could afford, and it was. Living fifty miles from my job would have never been a priority before our Stage 4 diagnosis but living on the water became a priority because we might not have been able to do it after retirement.

Living on Galveston Bay in that little 800-square-foot house was like being wrapped in a cocoon together. We spent hours every evening looking at the water and loved the sunrises and sunsets. We had wonderful family times when we rented the house next door and crammed both houses full of kids and grandkids for several days of laughter and fun.

Our priorities had changed completely, and our family made many wonderful memories of those times together.

God was working when he orchestrated finding our oncologist in Los Angeles. God knew that we would have a new publisher in Ventura and that we would spend many happy times there together.

God was working when my 86-year-old mom came to live with us at the bay the last three years of her life. She had dementia and was in a wheelchair, but she didn't have to be shut up in a house in Houston. She could sit for hours and enjoy the ocean with us.

God was working when he led us to a bigger home on the bay that would accommodate my mom. This house already had a bedroom and bath that had openings wide enough for her wheelchair to go through. Coincidence? I don't believe that for a minute.

God was working when our middle child, Shari, wanted to go to North Carolina with me on a speaking engagement, just one month before she was killed by a drunk driver. She was afraid to fly because it was just a month after 9/11, but her desire to be with me was stronger than her fear of flying. I have priceless memories that can never be taken away of spending those precious three days together. I will never believe this was a coincidence.

God was definitely working when He brought me back into John and Allyson's lives. I had been retired and widowed for five years when I received word that Allyson was no longer responding to treatment and that her cancer had spread over her body. For thirty years Allyson and I had stayed friends but saw each other infrequently for lunch with Joy and at family celebrations. However, we talked on the phone for many hours over the years. When I heard Allyson was going to begin ten days of brain radiation to alleviate severe headaches, nausea, and double vision. I called to see if I might drive her there.

My summer was free from teaching my First Place for Health class, and my schedule was pretty clear for the entire summer except for a week with our family at the beach in early July and a few days for our Annual FP4H event in August. My plan, originally, was to spend a few days with Allyson by taking her to her last four brain radiation treatments. After that first week, I began spending two to three nights a week in their home when John needed to be out of town on business.

Allyson and I talked for hours, filling in all the gaps of the past thirty years. When Allyson drove the cart at the grocery store for the first time, I loved seeing her excitement and joy. One day we got manicures and pedicures. We sat together outside in the evenings visiting with her wonderful neighbors, laughing together, watching silly TV shows.

Another day, Allyson reminded me of a phone conversation when she'd told me of her sadness about her mom's Alzheimer's diagnosis. Allyson remembered that I had said, "I'll be your mama during this time." I didn't remember the conversation, but I knew the Lord Jesus was using me to do what Allyson's mom would have been doing—loving and taking care of her.

While staying with Allyson, I walked in their neighborhood early each morning and loved the beautiful surroundings and sunrises. Bunny rabbits hopped around on my morning walks in their country surroundings. In town the most wildlife I see is a possum sitting on the top of a fence.

When I walked, I asked God why I was there. I loved being with John and Allyson, but this was something I had never done before and frankly, would have never thought of doing on my own. I knew that God had a plan, but I had no clue what it was. So I asked Him to reveal the plan to me.

I had never wanted to write about our journey through Stage 4 cancer and had always resisted my publisher when asked to do so. I was drawn into their story by love for John and Allyson and also my love for John's parents, Joy and Paul, who were 90 and 93. When Paul died, I was with Joy, helped make the funeral arrangements with John, wrote Paul's obituary, and travelled to Austin with John and Joy for Paul's funeral.

For three months I was in their home two to three days each week, and I was totally hooked by love for this entire family. I brought my cat, Big Boy, and moved into their home, telling John I was committed to being there for him as well as Allyson.

John is a prankster. He bought a big cow head mask, which he thought their two-year-old granddaughter, Payton, would love because they own a ranch with long-horn cattle. The first time he put it on his head, Payton screamed in terror. Allyson hid the mask and told John that it was hidden so well he would never find it. One day as he searched for the mask, John found one of Allyson's journals written two years earlier when Allyson was sad and angry about not seeing her grandkids grow up. I devoured the journal, astounded by the depth of Allyson's transparency in her writing. She wrote with a rawness I had never seen before, pouring out her broken heart to God. After reading those journal entries, I had to apologize to God for all the times I had failed to be honest in my writing to Him. I think I didn't want my children to see my pain or my wickedness, so I never wrote about it.

A few days later, John walked into the den with nineteen more journals. When I saw that stack of journals, I knew why I was there. God wanted me to tell Allyson and John's story and our story, too.

❧

I asked John if their priorities changed with the Stage 4 diagnosis.

Fifteen years ago, I had what I considered the best job in the city, working for the same dealer group for many years under the leadership of a friend and mentor named Mike Kelley. Mike guided me in so many circumstances, and I am forever grateful for his counsel. I leaned on him for wisdom related to work and personal life, and I always found his advice to be sound. Mike reached retirement age and made the announcement he was leaving, which was bittersweet for me. I would miss his presence at the dealership, but I also was being considered to replace him as General Sales Manager. Ultimately, the position was offered, and I accepted. I was humbled by the decision to hold this position and considered it my forever career.

The auto industry can be a challenging career. Two years into this new role of GSM, my experience with the store and the staff allowed me to navigate through the toughest of circumstances. The lifestyle it affords was wonderful. We took great vacations, lived in the best neighborhoods with the best schools, had nice cars, and eventually a pool for the boys to enjoy, but these perks came at a cost.

To meet various objectives from the manufacturer required many hours. I was working 60 plus hours a week and most Saturdays. Our everyday conversation was, "The boys are home, and you are at work. It's 8 o'clock. When will you be coming home?" My response was always the same. "As soon as I can wrap up the reports and make sure all deals are accounted for, I'll be headed home." Driving home and walking in the house long after it was dark was never pleasant. I would categorize it best this way: we endured. I felt Allyson needed a change of heart. She knew what was required of me and she should understand. I thought she would eventually come around and it would all work out. For 16 years, she endured.

Then Allyson was no longer willing to stay quiet. One evening I walked in the door and her demeanor was different. She had a way of communicating without saying a word, and I knew we were about to have a tough conversation. But being the car guy, I thought I could negotiate and win her back over. It would be ok. I just needed to let her say what she needed to say and let her know I understood how she felt. I would promise to make it all better. SOLD!

But she sold me that evening. Her argument was no longer about her needs, it was about our family. She explained the boys were in their formative years—one was in Junior High and the other just started High School. They needed a father close by, and they needed both of us. She told me about their challenges. I was not aware of them.

Mentally, I figured how I could carve off some time at work and spend more time at home. Maybe I could leave at seven instead of eight—another hour to be at home.

Then she got my attention. "I don't want you to live with regret. Our boys need you in their life, and if you are not willing to take drastic measures, you will live with regret the rest of your life." She won the negotiations that evening. I knew something had to change, but it would be walking away from a great career to make it happen.

After much prayer and wise counsel from men, I resigned my position. I considered many offers, turning down offers I never thought would come my way. The position I chose paid half of what I was making, and in many ways was a step down—a consultant role with a company that provided support to auto dealerships. I was starting all over again, but

I knew it was the right thing to do. What was most attractive to me was the company provided flexibility with schedule. My hours were long, but they were the hours I chose.

I later discovered this was the career for me all along. I made up the financial loss as I signed on new accounts. My schedule allowed me to be involved in the boys' lives, and I am still with the same company 15 years later. This opportunity was a blessing and what seemed to be a sacrifice and a step backwards actually made sense. If I had remained in the position at the dealership, I would have never known it was time to move one boy to a private school because he needed a new set of friends. I would not have had time to stay by Allyson's side during her last months of life. I worked at home, and the company gave me all the time I needed to be with her. I could attend to my mom after my dad passed away. I was with Allyson as she took her last breath.

Fifteen years ago, it made no sense for me to leave and take a significant pay cut and step into the unknown. Each night we prayed together for a new beginning, an open door, and the more we prayed, the more it made sense. It was strange to pray for an opportunity when I didn't want to leave my job. God guided our hearts to the right decision.

And one last comment: my granddaughter, Payton, stopped eating at Chick-fil-A because the posters on the wall were full of cow heads. Her soul is getting better.

Those with a Stage 4 cancer diagnosis have a unique opportunity to face life differently than they ever thought they would. To look at the world in a new way, to love more deeply, and to appreciate every minute they have left. This moment is a gift not one of us wants to receive. God was not taken by surprise by your Stage 4 cancer diagnosis, and He will be with you every step of the way. John says he would not be the man he is today if it were not for Allyson's cancer the last twenty-five years of their thirty-year marriage. He also said their sons would not be the men they are except for Allyson's cancer. Stage 4 changes everything, but it has the potential to change it for the better. I promise God cares about what you are going through, and He wants you to trust Him and know He is working on your behalf. God draws you close so He can walk this journey with you. Start looking for the ways He is at work in your life and thank Him for it.

Pray with Me

Dear Lord, I pray that we will welcome the change in priorities and that those areas that should have been priorities all along, like spouse and family and drawing close to You, will now take a place of importance. I thank You and praise Your Holy Name for the work You are going to do in all of our lives. In Jesus name, amen

Journal

Write about people and events that used to have top priority in your life. What priorities do you want to change to bring greater joy and peace?

Verse To Memorize

> "Trust in the Lord with all your heart and
> lean not on your own understanding; in
> all your ways acknowledge Him and He
> will make your paths straight"
> (Proverbs 3:5-6).

Allyson's Blog
Whom I Reflect Matters

It was a busy summer as usual this year. It began with me putting on my superwoman attitude that I could do all things. Not even a week had passed before I was exhausted and discouraged from trying to do too much. That doesn't surprise anyone who knows me. The new chemo wants to hold me to the couch like a magnet. I hate it, and I am grateful for it all in the same breath. The added laundry, meal planning, and puppy sitting were enough to juggle, and then it happened. The straw that brought this camel down. My husband got a cold—a nasty disgusting cold. If you are a wife reading this, I know you feel my pain. To make matters worse, while my husband was on his *death bed*, our ten-year-old lab twisted and tore the ligaments where his paw connects to his foot. I had always prided myself on being someone who would make logical decisions with my pets that would not be based on emotion. That theory was completely thrown out the window when challenged. After hearing my two options (and option one was not an option), I was easily persuaded he would need a very expensive surgery. Wives, if you ever need your husband to get out of their sick bed, tell him you scheduled your pet for an expensive surgery! It definitely got my husband moving.

Before you cast judgment, I came to my senses and opted to try a brace for our lab instead of surgery. At this point added to the extra laundry, dinners to cook, a puppy to watch, and a sickly husband, I now had a dog with a prosthesis to put on and take off throughout the day. There wasn't much time to read, reflect, or write because to do so would require I get some quiet uninterrupted time--and all of that time was spent asleep.

One day while I was whining to my mom about my added work load, recent lack of alone time, and the decline of my superwoman abilities, she replied with something profound. She said, "Honey, I thought you wanted to build a home rather than a house." She wasn't aware her words of wisdom rattled my crazy cage. While trying to keep the house running like a well-oiled machine, I had taken my eyes off what I really wanted my house to reflect. The rest of the summer, I tried to keep her words at the front of my mind and make the goal of building my home about enjoying and nurturing the relationships inside the home rather than being consumed with the appearance of the house.

Usually when I apply something in the physical sense, I look for a deeper spiritual lesson that I can apply. Under the banner of trying to take all things to God, I had fallen into the habit of asking God to make my days simpler. It seemed like the logical thing to do—to clean and tidy my problems, take away the drama, the stress, the physical issues, etc. so I could feel better, worry less, and do more.

To do what exactly I had no idea. My prayers revolved around removing all the obstacles I thought stood in my way. I am not implying this prayer is wrong, but it became wrong for me because it's all I was doing. I needed to redirect my reflection. Let me explain. My thoughts and my prayers reflect what my priorities are. It was subtle when it happened, but my priority had become me. Simply put, I have been reflecting me. Physically that's a given, but spiritually it's not the desire of my heart, nor is it pleasing to God. I had taken my eyes off who my face was reflecting.

Second Corinthians chapters 3-4 are very clear about who my face is to reflect—the face of Jesus. I had a veil over my face that distorted His image. It was made up of a maddening desire to please others, stressing over frivolous things, focusing on my inabilities, a bad attitude, and the dreaded *what ifs* to name a few. When this happens, the glory of who Jesus is becomes obscured and distorted. I couldn't see Him clearly but more importantly neither could those He placed in my path.

In these two New Testament chapters, Paul tells me that reflecting Jesus is my ministry at all times and in all situations. It's hardest for me to reflect Jesus when I'm physically drained, anxious, or disappointed, but those excuses are never an out. Anything that keeps others from clearly seeing Jesus in me acts as a veil that hides His glory. I hate the thought of hindering someone from seeing who He is.

Second Corinthians 3:17-18 commands us to live with unveiled faces that reflect Him daily, and this is a "no matter what" kind of message! It is a treasure to reflect the face of Jesus no matter what, and this alone allows for no discouragement to descend and remain upon my heart. Another rattle to my cage as I think of the many days I've wallowed in discouragement.

A godly friend said, "Sometimes God displays His power not by removing us from the problems but by showing us His sustaining power." How true and how grateful I am to have this opportunity to bear witness to His sustaining power. Now, rather than my priority being for God to resolve all my concerns, I ask Him to help my face reflect Jesus clearly with no distortion—because no one sees the beauty in a distorted image. I feel like if I get that right, my concerns will take their rightful place in the back seat rather than the front.

-Allyson

5

Circumstances Change

Our priorities need to change after a Stage 4 diagnosis but most of us don't expect circumstances to keep changing when we are dealing with something as huge as Stage 4. But this is life, and circumstances change frequently. During the first few years of Johnny's diagnosis, hard circumstances drove us deeper into our relationship with Jesus. God used every situation to make us stronger, so I thank Him for each one.

Johnny retired after his Stage 4 diagnosis. With our sudden move to the bay after John's home burned, I now drove 100 miles each day to and from work. Johnny, who was a fabulous cook, did all the grocery shopping and had our dinner ready every evening when I came home. After we cleaned up the kitchen, we still had several hours to sit on our pier. Life took on a much slower pace at the bay and it was like being on a perpetual vacation. Even though we were only an hour away from Houston, my phone rarely rang after I got home from work.

Two years after moving to our first tiny house on the water, my mom moved in with us. She had a series of TIAs, or mini strokes and dementia began taking over her brain. She was also in a wheelchair because of arthritis in her spine. She loved the water as much as we did and could spend hours on the pier just watching the ships pass through the ship channel. One day, we found a wonderful house on the water on almost an acre of property with 160 feet of waterfront. Our home in Houston sold to the State of Texas for the widening of the I10 freeway, so within a week we bought that house and now had plenty of room for lots of company.

Our kids and grandkids loved coming to the waterfront to play. For eleven 11 glorious years, we had days and days of fun we would not have experienced if we still lived in town. Our college age grandkids brought their friends to swim and play on our boat. Our daughter Shari, who was homeschooling her two youngest girls, came every time I had to leave town to take care of my mom and be there with Johnny.

For years Johnny cooked all the meals for our annual FP4H Wellness Week held at Round Top Retreat Center with the help of our two daughters, Lisa and Shari. After his Stage 4 diagnosis, our two daughters took over the cooking. After Shari's death in 2001, which I'll talk about in the next chapter, John's wife Lisa, our daughter-in-love, joined the cooking team. Today, our daughter-in-love does all the cooking for FP4H events with the help of her daughter, Harper.

Because Johnny had cooked for so many years at Round Top and so many of our FP4H people knew and loved him, it was natural to bring folks to the bay on Saturday afternoon after our Annual FP4H Summit at the end of July. We did that for nine years and hosted a group of 300 men and women just three weeks before Hurricane Ike.

We had to evacuate for Hurricane Ike. Euphanel and Nick Goad, who owned Round Top Retreat, texted, "come here." They rarely allow pets at the retreat center, so I texted back that we had our dog, Meathead, two cats, and a bird. They texted, "bring 'em on." We took little when we evacuated—Johnny's meds and a few clothes—because we intended to go back home the next day.

The storm came in at night on Friday the 13th with a seventeen-foot wall of water. That tidal surge came in and out of our home during the night. Our next-door neighbors drove to the bay and had to park two miles away as the road was flooded. When they got to our homes, they saw their home had minimal damage because it was up on pilings, but our home was destroyed. Melissa and Greg brought pictures to Round Top that night. Greg insisted Johnny and I live in their home at the bay until we could meet with all the insurance adjusters and decide what we were going to do.

We stayed at Round Top Retreat for five weeks, and it was wonderful. Groups meeting at the retreat felt so sorry for us they fed us the entire time. Our daughter Lisa set up an Excel spreadsheet for me to list the contents of our home. A friend had taken extensive pictures of every room in our home and made a notebook in case something like this happened. I could visually see what was in every room. Those five weeks were a big change in our circumstances, but God placed us at Round Top Retreat where He loved on us through so many caring believers. I will always be grateful that God prompted Euphanel Goad to text me that morning to "come here".

We moved into Greg and Melissa's home. Johnny rarely left the house, as it was difficult for him to climb the stairs.

It was depressing to see our beautiful home demolished with holes in every room. It was pitiful seeing our dog and the two cats wandering in and out of the debris.

We could have rebuilt, but Johnny asked me the perfect question, "Carole, if I'm not here, do you want to live full time at the bay?" I immediately said, "No, I'm here because you're here. If you aren't here, I want to live in Houston closer to the kids." Our circumstances had changed, but God knew that this was the next Stage of our journey, and He was committed to see us through it to the end.

A friend of mine from church was selling her townhouse in Houston, and it was completely furnished. I asked if she would consider renting it to us since we didn't have any furniture left from the storm. She took the townhouse off the market and told us to stay as long as we wanted. We lived in her townhouse for fifteen months and never wanted for a single thing. I fell in love with the neighborhood as several families from our church lived there as well.

We couldn't buy my friend's townhome because her bedrooms were all upstairs, and we needed a downstairs bedroom and bath for Johnny. A townhouse came up for sale that had a downstairs bedroom and bath, and we bought it. Our son, John, was between jobs as a contractor, so he hired two helpers who gutted the townhouse and totally remodeled it while we stayed in the rental. Three months later, we moved into a townhouse that looked brand new even though it had been built thirty-five years before.

We felt so blessed because we had insurance. Many people at the bay didn't have insurance, and they were living in tents in their yard. No matter how dire the situation, there is always so much to be thankful for if we will just look for it.

After we bought the townhouse, we also bought a used RV and put it on our property at the bay. We lived down there semi-permanently until a year before Johnny passed away. Johnny always chose to stay at the bay when I needed to travel. He was never bored or lonely on the water.

Our sixteen-plus years of living with Stage 4 cancer were some of the best years of our fifty-five-year marriage. We had the love of friends and family, and life was never dull. I wrote fifteen books during those sixteen years, thirteen of them after Shari's death in 2001, which was another huge change in our circumstances, but I'll tell you about that in the next chapter.

Allyson and John's circumstances changed many times

during Allyson's twenty-five-year cancer battle. They had two small children when Allyson was diagnosed with Stage 4 cancer, and she was working as an oncology nurse. After her Stage 4 diagnosis, she quit work and stayed home to raise her boys. Tyler is now 30 and married to Hannah with two little girls, Payton and Paisley. Ben is 27 and married to Brittainy and working at a great job after finishing college. John has been in the car business since college.

One day, as John and I drank our morning coffee on the patio, John said, "I've been in the car business for so many years and I know lots of people. My youngest, Ben doesn't care about my former life, but Tyler wants to know everything. When he meets someone I worked with years ago, he asks them to tell him about me back then. I told Tyler he will never find out anything I am ashamed of. Then he made the statement, "I am so grateful I never compromised my ethics, my morals or my faith." That a man who has had a wife with Stage 4 cancer for twenty-five years can say that is profound.

Allyson, being a stay-at-home mom, was a vital part of her boy's lives even when dealing with Stage 4 cancer. A few weeks before Allyson passed away, Ben said, "I never realized, growing up, how sick Mom was." John explained how Allyson never wanted her boys to have only memories of a mom with cancer. She might be throwing up her toenails from chemo and come out to have pizza with the boys and their friends. One time Ben wanted to have a sleepover and Allyson was throwing up in the bathroom. John said she shouldn't allow the sleepover. She said, "John, this is for me!"

Allyson was close to her parents and to her brother, Russell, who is ten years older. Allyson's mom was diagnosed with breast cancer just six months before Allyson's diagnosis but had remained cancer free for twenty-five years. Allyson's dad died from a serious injury following an automobile accident. Her mom remarried a wonderful Christian man who cared for her as she battled Alzheimer's.

Many young people came to visit Allyson because they loved her so much. Allyson had five close girlfriends who wanted to meet her every need when she was sick. Not many people can say this, but Allyson poured out her life to others while living with Stage 4 cancer. She left a huge legacy not only to her husband, John, but to her two sons and countless friends and mentees she loved over those twenty-five years.

Allyson and John never once blamed God for her Stage 4 cancer. They lived full lives and Allyson had many joy-filled years, even though her cancer returned twelve times. With the chemo, she lost her hair five times.

When Allyson was struggling, she asked me to pray with her. She told me her thoughts, her doubts, her hurts, and what she needed most. She was such a wonderful person, yet she expressed that she thought God was not pleased with her. Sounds strange to hear someone who walks the narrow path feel as if God is not pleased with her thoughts, but that was Allyson. She was not afraid to share her innermost thoughts. She said when I prayed with her, it lifted her spirit. She quoted James 5:16, "The prayer of a righteous man is powerful and effective." She knew I had flaws, but she also knew my heart was in tune with hers. She asked me often if I was praying for her. I would answer, "I am always praying for you. Every step I take, I am thinking about you and asking for God's favor." Every day, I was in conversation with God. It didn't matter where we were in this cancer journey, good reports, bad reports, my prayers were non stop and unyielding.

In the last few months of her life, I was available to be with her as much as I needed to be, which was a blessing. But seeing someone you love slowly fade is also troubling. For me, I loved rolling up my sleeves and doing everything I could to bring her comfort, but I realized I needed to be encouraged and strengthened with each passing day. During the last months, I started walking. I grabbed the leash, my Bose Soundsport ear pods, and headed out the door with my yellow lab, "Honeybear." What started out to be a 30-minute walk turned to an hour and twenty minute walk as I realized how much Casting Crowns, Big Daddy Weave, Hillsong, and other Christian groups lifted my spirits. Around 5:00 p.m. each day, I looked forward to getting alone with God. In addition to the long walks in the evening, I needed a word from the Lord. Allyson loved the Psalms because, like Allyson, David expressed every thought (both good and bad). One morning, I read Psalm 116, and I thought Allyson needed to hear it, so I walked into the room and read to her:

"I love the Lord because he hears my voice and my prayer for mercy. Because he bends down to listen, I will pray as long as I have breath! Death wrapped its ropes around me; the terrors of the grave overtook me. I saw only trouble and sorrow. Then I called on the name of the lord: 'Please, Lord save me!' How kind the Lord is! How good he is! So merciful, this God of ours!" (Psalm 116:1-5 NLT).

Allyson asked me to pray this Psalm as a prayer over her every day from then on. It was difficult for me to get through it without shedding tears, but it spoke to both of us.

❧

My friend Liz Henshaw lives in Vicksburg, Mississippi, and has lived for twenty-one years with Stage 4. Her circumstances changed recently when her son Michael, who was forty years old, was killed in a tragic automobile accident. I talked to Liz recently, and we both shared how the Stage 4 journey pales with the loss of one of our children. Here is Liz's story:

Liz Henshaw

It was Friday. I had been working from home that day waiting to hear from the doctor about my test results. He said he would call, and I was so excited when 5:00 p.m. rolled around and I had not heard from him. I sat down to enjoy the evening and await my husband Dan and son Patrick's return from a track meet. Then my phone rang, a phone call that changed everything in a single sentence, "I'm sorry to tell you but you have breast cancer." The fear was overwhelming. I screamed and cried and prayed. Dan did not have a cell phone so I could not call him. I called my best friend who lived a mile away, and she was at my house in an instant.

Earlier that year, a business associate noticed I was rubbing the side of my neck. I did not realize I was even doing it and had no idea how long the knot had been there. She encouraged me to see a doctor as soon as I returned to Houston. I took her advice. I could tell by the look on the doctor's face that she was concerned. She sent me for a CT scan and biopsy the next day as my concern turned to fear and anxiousness that I had never felt before.

Following the phone call, I called my sister so she could tell my mother in person. Within a few minutes, we were all on the phone together. And by the next morning, my mom and three sisters were at my back door.

I noticed my mother had three suitcases. I asked her why so many just for a few days and she responded, "I'll go home when you have recovered. Until then, I'm staying." A mother's love can be extraordinarily strong for her children, even when they are grown.

In the next week, I was tested from head to toe. The doctors were concerned because the cancer had left the primary site (breast) and had spread beyond the lymph nodes in my neck and underarm. This limbo time— waiting on test results—is one of the most difficult periods of dealing with cancer. The not knowing, the waiting, and the praying that I would receive the best medical care. Prayer and leaning on God in any challenge is what we do; but this seemed to bring another whole dimension to our lives.

I remember searching God's word through this early Stage of my journey and came upon Habakkuk 3:19,

"The Sovereign Lord is my strength; he makes my feet like the feet of a deer; he enables me to tread on new heights." This verse spoke to me in a new way; seeing God strengthen me with Him at my side. I remember seeing Jesus holding my hand across the river. And I also remember say- ing "Whether or not I survive this, Jesus is with me every step of the way".

After a battery of tests over three weeks, the diagnosis was Stage 4 breast cancer. I was then referred to an oncologist by the surgeon. Although the surgeon wanted to do surgery first and fast because the mass in my breast was 4.5 centimeters by 4.5 centimeters, he wanted me to see the oncologist first; thank God. This was a turning point in my care.

At our first oncology appointment, I was greeted by a male nurse, who came out to introduce himself and said, "Mrs. Henshaw before we do anything, can I please pray with you?" I could not believe it: God's hand at work right there in the waiting room at the clinic. After the nurse prayed with us, he said, "Prayer is important for two reasons. Number one, I believe in the power of prayer but number two, I wanted to thank God for you and for you being our patient with Dr. Valero." I didn't understand what he meant. He continued, "Dr. Valero is not taking any more patients. But when he saw your chart, he wanted to take care of you." God answers prayers before we pray them. Dr. Valero was on loan to this clinic. He was a breast oncologist specialist from MD Anderson. My insurance did not cover MD Anderson, but they covered the clinic.

"He gives strength to the weary and increases the power of the weak. Even youths grow tired and weary, and young men stumble and fall; but those who hope in the Lord will renew their strength. They will soar on wings like eagles; they will run and not grow weary, they will walk and not be faint" (Isaiah 40:29-31).

My greatest desire during this ordeal was to protect my family. Dr. Valero explained the aggressive treatment protocol. I told him that was fine with me because I would not die because I still had children at home. Patrick was about to start the 8th grade and Michael had recently graduated high school. I wanted to see these boys graduate college, get married, have children of their own, and I wanted to become a grandmother.

My cancer was HER2-Positive and the success rate for this type of cancer was generally not good. The protocol required four rounds of chemotherapy therapy and then retesting to see if the tumor had responded to the chemotherapy by shrinking. Now remember, the surgeon wanted to do surgery first. And the oncologist wanted to do chemotherapy first. After four rounds of chemotherapy, I understood why the oncologist wanted to do treatment first. Had we done surgery first, we would have had no way to test the size of the tumor to see if it was responding to the chemotherapy. My tumor did not respond.

Chemotherapy was brutal. Nausea, loss of appetite, mouth sores, hair loss (which happened on Mother's Day), sleepless nights, and so many other problems. But through all of this, I had an amazing team of doctors, nurses, family, friends, and Sunday School class members. God continued to show his mercy and give me strength every day. The Bible says, "Do not be anxious about anything but in everything, by prayer and petition, with Thanksgiving, present your requests to God. And the peace of God which transcends all understanding, will guard your hearts and your minds in Christ Jesus" (Philippians 4:6-7). Even while anxious, I kept my faith and trusted God would see me to the other side of the river with Him, no matter what. A peace settled on me that truly surpassed all understanding.

The first four rounds of chemotherapy had done nothing to shrink the tumor or affect the lymph nodes. Hearing this news was the first time I thought I was in real trouble. And it crossed my mind that I might die. Dr. Valero told me about a new drug that had just come out of clinical trial. He prescribed Taxotere and Herceptin. Herceptin was the new drug. I asked, "Would you give this to your wife?" and he said, "Absolutely." We started another chemotherapy protocol the next week with these new drugs.

During my treatments, my husband Dan was named the Lysol King. He would not allow anyone to come into the house unless they changed clothes in the laundry room (he had extra clothes and bathrobes for visitors), and they had to spray down with Lysol. We laugh about that now when we look back, but I never contracted any illness during my 12 months of treatment.

As treatments built up in my body, I became weaker and weaker. There were days I could not get to the bathroom by myself. I did not have the strength to walk up and down the stairs. I was scheduled for another series of follow-up tests but did not have the strength to walk. For a few days I was in a wheelchair. I'd had a reaction to a medicine that controlled hot flashes and one of the side effects was loss of leg movement. When they figured out the cause, I soon walked again.

The new drugs proved to be the right weapon. After four more rounds, the tumor and lymph nodes shrank. The doctor felt like the time was right for the surgery.

And Mom never left me. Dan had never cooked (and still doesn't to this day) so my mother kept us fed and healthy with all her home cooking during that year.

Following surgery, I had a six-week break from any treatment and got to enjoy Christmas with my family before I started radiation, another brutal experience.

Cancer is not a death sentence, but it took me a while to grasp that idea. Maintaining a positive attitude, trusting in God, letting others help you, and staying involved in your medical care are key components to recovery. I have been cancer free 20 years and often look back and wonder "why?" While I may never understand, I know the year I spent with my mother was precious. Many memories are good. And I learned God is in control. He walked me through whatever I was facing each day. Treatments and protocols tested by brave women before me benefitted me. Herceptin, the drug that saved my life, came out of clinical trials right when I needed it. A radiation study proved that radiation vs. stem cell created a better chance of survival. I am grateful for all those women who risked the trials and sacrificed for the development of new drugs and treatment protocols.

I don't know how people manage major events in their life without Christ. God told Joshua, "Be strong and courageous. Do not be frightened, and do not be dismayed, for the Lord your God is with you wherever you go" (Joshua 1:9). And I know Christ was with me every day, the good days and the bad ones.

~Liz Henshaw

෴

Your life is not over till it's over. It's your choice whether you fight for life or give in to death. Life goes on. Live it every day you awake. Circumstances will change but you will continue to go deeper with God because of those changes. God will give you the grace and strength to do it if you trust Him and place your fragile life in His hands.

Pray With Me

Dear Lord, I don't know the changing circumstances we will face on top of the Stage 4 journey, but You do, and that's all that matters. I pray that You will show us that You are in the middle of all these changing circumstances if we will only look for You. In Jesus' name, amen.

Journal

Are there other pressing circumstances going on besides the Stage 4 journey? Write them out in detail, asking God to take charge and give you wisdom.

Verse To Memorize

"Do not be anxious about anything, but in everything, by prayer and petition, with thanksgiving, present your requests to God. And the peace of God, which transcends all understanding, will guard your hearts and your minds in Christ Jesus" (Philippians 4:6-7).

Allyson's Blog
And God Said, "Let There Be Light."

We make such a big deal about the first words our children speak. "Dada. Mama. Or my son's first word, "No!"

Should I not make a bigger deal about the first words spoken by The Creator of the Universe? God's first recorded spoken words were, "Let there be light." He had revealed Himself as "Elohim" Creator God in Genesis: 1-2 by creating the heavens and the earth. But he ushered in light with the power of His spoken word. We know from other passages that God himself radiated light, so it wasn't that He needed to illuminate His way. The life He would later create to sustain itself would need light, but there is a deeper spiritual symbolism to be seen.

God never intends for us to live in darkness, not physical—but even more—not spiritual.

In John 8:12, Jesus speaks to the unbeliever when He says, "I am the light of the world. Whoever follows me will never walk in darkness but will have the light of life." This beautiful invitation by the Savior Himself for unbelievers is the most important lesson here, but there is a message for the believer as well.

If you have ever been in a pit of emotional darkness, you feel so alone. Key word in that statement is "feel."

We are physically seen, but we feel emotionally hidden from the world and at times from God as well. I felt this aloneness in the summer of 2004. Overnight a virus swept through my right inner ear, leaving me with complete hearing loss and a damaged balance center. I was unsteady, uncomfortable in public places, unable to locate where sounds were coming from, and heard a constant roaring in my ear. I was most comfortable at home, alone. I questioned why God would allow this on top of the cancer I was already battling.

I immersed myself in the Book of Psalms, as I had done many times before. It was as if I was reading it for the first time, and the prayers of David gradually became my own. In Psalm 13, it is easy to see that David felt forgotten by God. His thoughts were a battleground, and his heart was full of sorrow. After confessing his honest feelings to God through prayer, David says: "But I trust in your unfailing love; my heart rejoices in your salvation. I will sing to the Lord, for He has been good to me" (Psalm 13:6). After all the raw emotions David had expressed, I wondered how could he claim The Lord had been good to him?

The goodness David saw was not the circumstances his

earthly life had given him, but rather the saving and unfailing love God had for him. Simply put, knowing God and being His was enough for David. I prayed it would be enough for me.

God's character and nature are revealed to us in the names given to Him throughout the Bible. One of those names is "El Roi" meaning the "God who sees." Nothing escapes Him. His Word confronts our feelings with the truth that all darkness is as broad daylight to Him.

When you feel you are in a dark place, I pray you will hear Him speaking into your situation, "Let there be light."

"Your Word is a lamp to my feet and a light for my path" (Psalm. 119:105).

"Who among you fears the Lord and obeys the word of his servant? Let him who walks in the dark, who has no light, trust in the name of the Lord and rely on his God" (Isaiah 50:10).

"I will be glad and rejoice in your love, for you saw my affliction and knew the anguish of my soul" (Psalm 31:7).

~Allyson

6

Making Sense of It All

You will never make sense of this Stage 4 diagnosis unless you get your relationship with God where it needs to be. You may be like I was. Everything looked great on the outside but when I was hit with a traumatic event, I didn't have the power to muscle through it without God's help.

I would not be the person I am today without the trials I've experienced.

On Thanksgiving morning, I woke very early. My habit was to get up at 4 a.m. and spend an hour with the Lord before driving into Houston. But this morning was not a workday. It was Thanksgiving, and we had 30 people coming for lunch. I lay still as I argued with God about getting up but after about ten minutes I was wide awake, so I went to the kitchen to start the coffee. While the coffee was brewing, I opened my Bible to James 1. I read through the chapter a couple of times while the coffee was making and never gave it another thought. James wrote, "Count it all joy when you face various trials for you know the testing of your faith develops perseverance and perseverance must finish its work so you may be mature and complete, not lacking anything." The last verse of that chapter is James 1:27 which says, "Religion that God our Father accepts as pure and faultless is this: to look after orphans and widows in their distress and to keep oneself from being polluted by the world."

In those early hours of Thanksgiving morning, I did not know it would be the day our 39-year-old daughter, Shari, would leave this world after being struck and killed by an 18-year-old girl who was driving drunk.

Shari and Jeff and their three girls had spent Thanksgiving Day with us, and Shari had decorated my Christmas tree before they left to have dinner with Jeff's parents. As they prepared to leave, Shari remembered something in the trunk of their Expedition. She jumped out as her mother-in-law walked out to the car to retrieve the items. The two women were standing behind the car talking when Christen, Shari's 15-year-old middle daughter, got out of the car to put a pie she was holding into the trunk. As the three of them stood there, a car left the street and barrelled down the sidewalk toward them. Cara, the oldest at 19 saw the car and said, "Oh God, don't let me be the only one left alive in my family." The out-of-control car hit a light pole and ricocheted, hitting Shari.

A few hours later, Shari left us for heaven during surgery. Jeff said he felt as if he had been in training during their twenty years of marriage to finish the raising of their three daughters. He told the girls, "In the morning, we will still believe the same thing about God we believed this morning." Jeff set the tone for all of us with that statement. God showed up in might and power during that sad time.

Our lives were forever changed when Shari was taken from us. We thought Johnny's Stage 4 cancer was the worst that could happen, but even worse is for a child to die before their parent. When Shari woke that Thanksgiving morning, she entered Stage 4 of her life and didn't know it. How many people are in Stage 4 in their marriage and don't have a clue? How many are in Stage 4 with their health but are clueless that they will die an early death from diabetes, heart attack or stroke, because they have neglected taking care of themselves?

Life will go on for you and there will be lots of unplanned events on top of your Stage 4 cancer diagnosis. Some of those will be wonderful and some will be extremely painful because this is life. If we live long enough, there will be suffering. Johnny and I had grown children when he was diagnosed and John and Allyson had very young children. Your situation will differ from ours because it is your life.

So how do we make sense of it all when we are dealing with a Stage 4 diagnosis but also with our change of priorities, circumstances, and life events? I have had years to ponder this question, and I can only come up with two words: *But God*. God led Johnny to desire a home on the water before his diagnosis with Stage 4. God was there at the time of the dreaded diagnosis. He was there when we chose a treatment plan. He was there when my mom came to live with us. He was there when our daughter Shari was killed. He was there when my mom left for heaven. He was there when Hurricane Ike destroyed our home. He was there when we moved back to Houston. He was there when we entered the final stretch of Johnny's life and there when He called Johnny home.

Being on this side of these events, I see the hand of God

leading us each step of the way. As I look back on the day our daughter died, I realize the Lord woke me early so He could spend time with me. Leading me to open my Bible to James 1 and read it a couple of times was a precious way of letting me know we were going to face a trial before the day ended. The Lord Jesus was already grieving for us about what we would face that night. I am forever grateful that I got up after He woke me and spent time with Him before that day unfolded.

In the two weeks after Shari's death, I saw God's hand everywhere and being a writer, I jotted down every time I had something else to be thankful for. I knew I was in shock, so I didn't want to forget how God showed up during our time of intense grief. Later I wrote a book, *A Thankful Heart,* from that list of twenty-two notes I jotted down during that two-week period.

Shari's death started me thinking about what it means to leave a legacy when we leave this world at a younger age than most. Shari didn't know she would die at thirty-nine years old, but God did. God knows before we take our first breath when we will take our last. He hard-wired Shari to have no greater desire than to marry and have children. She absolutely adored being a mom. At her memorial service, it was said that those three girls had more love in their young lives than most have if they live to 90.

My Mother passed away at 89 and what a legacy she left to me. My publisher wanted me to write a book on grieving because of Johnny's cancer and the death of our daughter and my mom. I told them I didn't feel led to write that book, but I could write a book about legacy. Our oldest granddaughter, Cara and I co-wrote, *The Mother Daughter Legacy* while Cara was a student at Texas A & M University. The book is about the legacy a mom passes to her child—the legacy my mom passed to me, which I passed to my children and Shari passed to her three girls. Legacy is the way we live on in the lives of those we love.

Our children were all grown with children of their own when Johnny was diagnosed with Stage 4 at fifty-eight years old. As I have reflected on the legacy he left, there are so many places I see his mark. Both of our girls were fabulous cooks, and after Shari died, our oldest daughter, Lisa, put together a legacy cookbook for every member of our family. It has Johnny's favorite recipes, along with Shari's favorites and some of my mom's recipes as well. Now, Lisa's oldest son Carl carries on the legacy of preparing beautiful foods for himself and others to enjoy. I know Johnny would absolutely love seeing the pictures Carl posts on social media of the delicious foods he prepares.

I vividly remember a day when our great grandson

Luke was at the bay when we were living in the RV after Hurricane Ike. Johnny had an uncanny knack for spotting athletic ability in young children. He nailed it in our son John when he was a 2-year-old and spent hours pitching a ball for John to bat when he was still a toddler. Johnny saw that same ability in Luke, and as weak as he was, went outside to pitch balls for Luke to hit for probably an hour. Luke loved Johnny and not long before Johnny died, Luke pulled up a chair beside his bed, "Dampy, I need to tell you something." Luke explained he would not play baseball the next season because he was going to ride dirt bikes with his dad. Johnny told Luke he had his blessing to ride dirt bikes instead of playing baseball. After Johnny's passing, Luke went through Johnny's many T-shirts and picked some to keep. His aunt Christen made pillows of the T-shirts, and he still has them on his bed. The first time I spent the night at their home after Johnny's death, Luke brought me one of those T-shirt pillows to have in bed with me. This is legacy. Helping another to be their best self and blessing their efforts, whatever they are.

Allyson was diagnosed at twenty-eight years old with two young boys. With Stage 4, Allyson knew there was a possibility that she might not live to see her boys reach adulthood. Allyson poured her life into her marriage and mothering. She wrote letters to her boys beginning in elementary school—page after page teaching them, encouraging them, and loving them on paper—and the boys answered. She wanted her boys to remember her words and her presence in their lives. Ben said when he got up in the morning, the notebook might be slipped under his door with a message his mom had written the night before. When the boys wrote Allyson back, they always said, "Write me back."

Both of the boys grew up with their mom fully engaged in their lives and their desire today is for their own wives to stay home and raise their children the way they were raised. These boys never knew what it was like for their mom to not have Stage 4, but they never felt neglected because of it. Allyson left a legacy of love that will never die.

❦

Ben Wrote a Few of His Thoughts

My mom used letters to communicate with me all the time. She would leave them in my room and often write additional letters even if I had forgotten to write her back. Later on, we ended up realizing we communicated well that way, and I remember if we had an argument, we would often "text" it out in how we were feeling.

A few months before she passed away, she was not feeling well and was up and down emotionally, which was unlike her. She has always been stable and consistent. She was different because she knew she was not far away from leaving us. I could tell she was upset because she felt like she had no more energy left to see people and spend time with anyone. She was physically and mentally exhausted from the treatment and from the cancer itself. I let her know it was okay to relax, and for once in her life, focus on herself and doing what is best for her. We watched a sermon together that night. It was a little after midnight and I had just gotten into bed when I heard a knock on my door. Mom found the energy to use a walker and come all the way over to my room to let me know what she wanted to be remembered by … which was someone who trusted and loved God with all of her heart and not someone who would be up and down emotionally but consistent in her faith in God. I let her know it was okay because she was having tough moments. She had been fighting for twenty-five years, and it was only getting tougher, but she wanted me to know that she did not want to be stressed or remembered for emotional ups and downs.

As I reflected on the letters she wrote me and the reasons why she wrote I first thought she did it knowing that she would leave me something behind. However, I now feel that it was God's plan for me to have those letters to reflect on. I believe my mom wrote letters to me because it was a way to write out her emotions and also a way to communicate to me on a more intentional level. Even though I did not always write my mom back, I kept every letter.

Once, I texted my mom saying that I hated she had to go through this. She responded with, "I know … 'All things God will work for the good of His people.' I know He has already done that but I'm sure there is more to come."

One night when I was staying with my mom I remember asking her if it was difficult that she could not read or study the Bible anymore and she told me that although she wished she could still study the Word she had studied it for so many years that she knew scriptures and it was in her heart. So even though she could not read it anymore, she remembered God's promises through the difficult times.

&

Shari's death was sudden, so she had no time to contemplate the legacy she would leave. But she left one, nevertheless. One of the gifts of Stage 4 is that you have time to think about the legacy you want to leave. You may live many years as Johnny and Allyson did, with the opportunity to be very intentional in the way you live.

My prayer is that you will ask the Lord Jesus to help you make sense of it all. Ask Him to show you the next step to take. I live my life by the statement, "Do the next right thing". What is the next right thing for you to do today?

Pray With Me

Dear Lord, I pray You will open our minds and heart right now.. Help us make sense of where we are today and show us the next right thing to do and give us the strength to do it. In Jesus' name, amen.

Journal

Write some ideas you might have about how you can begin leaving a legacy for those you love. What can you change that you no longer need to be doing? What can you add that will bless you and your friends and loved ones?

Verse to Memorize

"Don't collect for yourselves treasures
on earth, where moth and rust destroy
and where thieves break in and steal. But
collect for yourselves treasures in heaven,
where neither moth nor rust destroys and
where thieves don't break in and steal. For
where your treasure is, there your heart
will be also" (Matthew 6:19-21).

Allyson's Blog
Grace

New vehicles today have so many advanced ways to help keep us out of *avoidable* accidents. My new favorite is the caution light in the side mirrors to warn me not to change lanes. Another one that I can't decide if it's helpful or just goofy is the vibrating seat. If you cross over the white line without putting on your blinker to change lanes, the seat vibrates to alert you. It will either vibrate on the left or the right depending which side you cross that line. I can't believe technology has come so far. Not to mention front crash alert to keep you from getting too close to a car, and all the backup sensors. Really? I make fun of the technology, but I love it too. The idea is to prevent varied accidents, but as my son pointed out, they also make us mentally lazy if we rely solely on all these gadgets to make us safer drivers.

The last few months, God has been layering on my knowledge about living within His grace, and He quite often uses simple illustrations to drive home a deep truth. How does that relate to the vibrating alerts in my car? It doesn't really, except I feel like I'm constantly moving in and out of the lane of grace God has laid before me. I wish I had something to jolt me back before I cross all the way over, cruising down the lane of legalism, performance-based faith, and unknowingly trying to earn the favor of God.

I recently realized I was cruising in this lane when I was being brutally honest with a dear friend and these words came out of my mouth, "I'm exhausted spiritually and physically from trying so hard to maintain a strong faith. I need a spiritual vacation!" The alerts went off, and I heard that heart whisper, *you aren't walking in My grace.* That's all He said. That's really all He needed to say. He wanted me to ponder on grace. Pondering is a good thing because it gives God time to show and tell.

After God had told me this, He showed me a fresh example of what it looked like to live in His grace when I was visiting a friend who had recently adopted a toddler. God used the two-year-old to speak a fresh word. Her environment before her adoption was described to me as one that met her necessary needs, but that was where it ended. It sounded like a cold, crowded, sterile type of environment where there wasn't nearly enough affection to go around. How could she possibly be expected to embrace so much love from her new parents? Yet, she did. God wanted me to see the beauty of the unhindered mind of this child, which freed her to embrace this unconditional new love from her adoptive parents. When

I allow my mind to become hindered with what is out of my control, it leads me to feeling burdened, and feeling burdened leads to fatigue.

This is why Jesus says in Matthew 11:28-30, *"Come to me."* The message could stop right there with those three lifesaving words, but He adds; *"all you who are weary and burdened, and I will give you rest. Take my yoke upon you and learn from Me, for I am gentle and humble in heart, and you will find rest for your souls. For my yoke is easy and my burden is light."*

The yoke of Christ is the cross, which is also the vehicle He used to extend grace to me and to you. He paid the highest price to offer me grace. Simply put, He says, *Come to Me, receive My grace and your soul will rest.*

Operating outside of His grace whether it's an hour or a month is exhausting because it becomes all about me and my striving. My mind so easily and unknowingly becomes hindered on a daily and hourly basis. Doubts, fears, busyness, among a few things, jump in and interrupt my mind's thoughts on how very much my God loves me. He sees and is patient with my doubts. He sees and understands my every fear voiced or unvoiced, and He knows the fatigue that comes from a busy week. He doesn't want me to wear myself out trying to prove anything. He wants me to find the rest available in His grace and gain strength in knowing this grace is all I need. See 2 Corinthians 12:9.

My friend's new daughter was soaking up all the love available to her. She didn't wake up in the morning wondering if the love had gone, nor did she worry throughout the day if she was doing anything wrong to hinder the love her new parents had for her. She simply received every bit of love coming her way, no questions asked. God could not have used a more perfect example to show me what living in His grace looks like. Quite a contrast to the worn-out individual screaming for a vacation. I don't need nor want a spiritual vacation, but I needed a reminder that my relationship with Him is based on grace. I can do nothing more to earn His love. It's there every morning, all throughout the day, despite my shortcomings. It's always there.

~Allyson

7

Heart Care

The Bible tells us that the heart is the center of the mind, will, and emotions. Dealing with Stage 4 cancer will create havoc with our mind, will, and emotions unless we relinquish control of our lives and ask God to take charge. The Bible says in Jeremiah 17:9, "The heart is deceitful above all things and beyond cure. Who can understand it?"

How do you incorporate other trials into your already full life? It is a huge interruption, as are most big events in life. Think about it. How many traumatic life events have we gone through that were planned? I can say for sure that I would not be the strong woman that I am today without those unplanned events.

Something happened 13 years before Johnny's Stage 4 diagnosis that, without it, I would have never made it. God used this tragedy to bring me to the end of myself and change my heart so that I was strong enough to take on Johnny's care, the care of my mom the last three years of her life, losing Shari to a drunk driver, and the loss of everything we owned when our home was destroyed by Hurricane Ike.

It is of the utmost importance that you look into where your heart is right now. Is your mind clear and focused, or is it a muddled mess? Is your will in line with whatever God's will is for this Stage 4 challenge or is it stubbornly telling God what He has to do for you? Are your emotions, even though going crazy, trusting God for your future or are you frantically fluctuating from tears to anger or self-pity?

The first gigantic hurdle Johnny and I faced was the failure of his forklift company during the downturn in the oil industry. Everything was going great until business dried up overnight. Companies were not buying material handling equipment and were not repairing the equipment they owned until it was urgent. We limped along financially, trying to pay the rent and the salaries of our two mechanics. Our youngest son was in college, so finances seemed impossible. We finally closed the company and declared bankruptcy. It was devastating, and I will never forget.

Johnny had refinanced the cars to make the interest payments on the forklifts that weren't selling, so we lost our cars, but we kept our home because of the homestead laws in Texas. I was working at our church and a friend picked me up and brought me home from work for a year. God was breaking my stubborn will a little at a time, but I was such a carnal Christian that I thought God must want to change Johnny. God knew I would never make it without His control and leadership in my life, so He kept tightening the screws until He got my attention.

God allowed bankruptcy because He had good plans for my life. God needed all of me. I was a believer, but I lived my life like I was saying, "God, You take care of heaven, and I'll take care of earth." I'll never forget sitting in a worship service at my church when I was at the lowest point I had ever been. Our pastor preached a sermon on the will that morning. He said, "God is a perfect gentleman and will not come in to do the needed work on your stubborn will without your permission. If you are not willing for God to come in you can pray this prayer, "Lord, I'm not willing but I'm willing to be made willing."

I was on staff at my church, so I hid the train wreck my life had become. I didn't go forward for prayer but as sincerely as I ever prayed a prayer, I prayed that prayer, "Lord, I'm not willing but I'm willing to be made willing." And I finished the prayer with, "And please don't let it hurt too bad." God changed me from the inside out because of that horrific experience. He broke my stubborn will and rebuilt me completely. I am convinced that I would have never become the director of First Place for Health or written the books He has helped me write if we had not declared bankruptcy. I'm so grateful to live in a country where you can recover from traumatic life events. We could work hard and become financially stable again before Johnny's Stage 4 diagnosis. In fact, God blessed our finances more than we deserved, as we gave Him first place in everything.

You will never make sense of this Stage 4 diagnosis unless you get your relationship with God where it needs to be. Everything looked great on the outside, but when I was hit with a traumatic event, I didn't have the power to muscle through it without God's help.

Stage 4 men and women who care for their heart (mind, will, and emotions) use their disease to bless others. My friend, Ken Lowrimore began a ministry at our church that has grown to include people from our city and others who are here for cancer treatment from all over the world. Here are Ken's words:

બ્સ

Ken Lowrimore

Five years into my Stage 4 cancer journey, I felt the Lord leading me to begin a cancer support group at my church. After receiving permission and encouragement from our staff, we began and we have seen this ministry grow over the years. Each month, 60-80 men and women attend our CanHope meeting for a meal, testimony, and prayer time together.

It has been a blessing for Sara and me to see God grow this ministry. At 82, I sensed God leading me to ask a young deacon if he would walk with me to become the facilitator of CanHope. Brad Simcik agreed and became the facilitator, and I have been acting as a consultant. Sara and I have developed many close relationships with fellow cancer travelers. We plan to continue until

God calls us home, or we become incapacitated.

Another friend, Melissa, has used her Stage 4 diagnosis to begin a Facebook prayer ministry to many who come to MD Anderson for cancer treatment. Melissa began meeting people while she was there for chemo and radiation. She learned their stories, prayed for them, and asked others to pray for them. Melissa is in remission now, but she continues this ministry and brings many from out of town to our monthly CanHope meeting.

The healthiest thing we can do to care for our heart is to get outside of ourselves and bless someone else.

Pray With Me

"Dear Lord, You know the contents of my heart. We ask You to reveal what's inside and heal those areas where my thinking is not in line with Yours. Bring my mind, will and emotions to a place of peace and submission to Your will. In Jesus' name, amen.

Journal

Make a list of all the thoughts that have invaded your mind since your diagnosis. Beside each entry, write the opposite thought. For example: Fear – Trust, Anger – Peace, Doubt – Faith.

Verse To Memorize

"The Lord does not look at the things man looks at. Man looks at the outward appearance, but the Lord looks at the heart" (1 Samuel 16:7b).

Allyson's Blog
Pulling Up The Bad Roots

James 5:16 tells us to confess our sins and pray for each other so that healing may come. Whether it's physical or emotional healing that my body needs, confession is just as much of a need for my soul as the need for prayer.

For the last couple of months, I have been trying to recover from a rib fracture and now I've injured it again. I wish I could say it was from doing something fun, but it wasn't. I was coughing. I have had a mysterious cough for months, and my weakened bones gave out.

I feel like life keeps throwing me one challenging hurdle after another. When physical pain and fatigue join up with the feeling that there are a lot of demands on my time and energy, the perfect storm blows up on my radar. I have been more than frustrated. I started out a few months back praying about it and asking God to help me. But when things didn't improve quickly enough, I gave up on that and just got irritated. I learned even a small amount of unresolved bitterness with what God has allowed in my life can take root and blossom into a lot of ugly. Negativity piled up like dirty laundry and my attitude was smelling bad.

The verse that caught my attention was Hebrews 12:15, which says, "See to it that no one misses the grace of God and that no bitter root grows up to cause trouble and defile many." I can assure you over the past few weeks God's grace has not been evident to some that have crossed my path because I was nurturing a bitter root. I gave in to the complaining and negativity and quickly became someone I didn't like. Let's be honest, people don't like to be around negative people, but I was stuck with myself. The fruit of a Spirit filled life such as compassion, patience, kindness, and gentleness with others had spoiled.

One evening while I was ranting my usual complaints to John, the lightbulb came on. You know the one I'm talking about. The one that you'd rather turn off because it lights up those areas you don't like to see. It directed the light to the real source of my exaggerated problems. It was me. It wasn't the demands on me (those really hadn't changed). It wasn't even the new physical problems because I always have something going on in that area of my life. What had changed was my attitude. Sad how quickly, but even sadder how a sour attitude could morph me into a miserable person overnight. When the light of God's word revealed the real problem was within, I knew no change on the outside could make it better.

The change had to come from within. I needed to purge myself of some ugly rotten fruit.

When I worked as a nurse, each morning I would prepare the IV bags for infusions by purging them. Flushing the air out of the lines with the saline solution is a must before connecting them to the patient. Just like those IV bags, I had accumulated a lot of negative air that needed to be flushed out with a big bag of God's grace so I could change what was flowing out of me and onto others. As usual, I went for a walk and confessed my frustrations. That word sounds nicer than using the sin word. The peace of God washed over me like a warm bath, forgiving me, and making me keenly aware of His presence. As His own, I am never left alone to cope. Yet for a few weeks, I was speaking and living like I was an orphan. He still only calls me to live one day at a time—one of my biggest challenges, by the way. I think I've journaled that a thousand times.

Something I read resonated with me. "We have to do more than just decide to have a better attitude, we have to manage this decision." I knew God wanted me to read those words. It's one thing to decide to change a behavior, it's another thing to maintain that decision. I make it a priority to maintain so many other areas of my life that pale compared to my attitude. Rarely do all those other areas have a direct effect on the people in my life, but my attitude affects everyone, especially those closest to me.

Each day, we need to make the adjustments necessary to keep our attitudes right. As in other areas in my life where I decide to change for the better often in a few weeks' time, I am right back to my old behaviors because I failed to make those small daily adjustments that have a big effect on my overall outcome for change. I have taken the right steps toward a better attitude, but for me to keep the momentum, I must stay mindful of any daily adjustments I need to make to avoid the negative trap and prevent that bitterness from taking root and flourishing into another ugly tree. For me, this means I need to be more aware of what I allow into my head throughout the day. What and who I listen to affects my emotions and my thoughts. Next, I need to be mindful of what I allow to enter and set up camp in my heart. "Taking my thoughts captive" as 2 Corinthians 10:5 says and making them obedient to Christ before they have time to take root. When something is taken captive, it is restrained, not allowed to run free. I had been allowing my negativity to run free. I'm paying more attention to what comes out of my mouth and if the two steps above are in check, then this should be easier because I know what I say with my mouth reflects what has taken root in my heart.

I am grateful God used Hebrews 12:15 to direct the light to what I needed to see and even though confession is not pleasant, it is healing.

Psalm 119:130 "The unfolding of Your words give light."

~ Allyson

8

Soul Care

Thriving with Stage 4 is possible when we see that God can use this disease for our good and for His glory. You met Ken Lowrimore in the last chapter. He has lived 25 years with Stage 4. He is a living testimony of what it means to care for your soul. I don't know how anyone can make it through Stage 4 without faith in Christ. I asked Ken to share some of his experiences.

Ken's Story

At the end of my third bout with NHL, I was told about an alternative treatment to build my immune system in Tijuana, Mexico. I called the hospital in Mexico and was given the names of 8 patients from different parts of the U.S. who had gone through the treatment. We travelled to San Ysidro, California, which is just across the border from the hospital. There was a hotel in San Ysidro that had an arrangement with the hospital in Mexico to transport cancer patients staying at the hotel across the border the next day. When I arrived in California, I could only do five pushups because my body was so weak from chemo. When I left four weeks later, after receiving 20 injections, I could do 55 pushups. Quite an improvement. The doctor told me they could not cure me of lymphoma, but they would inject vitamins, enzymes, and another ingredient that was healthy for the immune system. After each 20-minute treatment, I was treated to a healthy breakfast at the hospital.

Our time in Tijuana receiving alternative care was a blessing. We were getting good stuff into our bodies, and everyone was cheerful. We developed friendships with the 20 patients who were receiving treatment. After about a week, Sara received some injections for arthritis. One morning at the breakfast table, we noticed a young man crying. He and his wife were from the "bush" near Alaska. I had met Tony in the treatment room and went over to his table. He said, "Ken, I don't want to die from this stomach cancer." I asked his permission to ask him a couple of questions, "Tony have you come to that place in your spiritual journey that you know you would spend eternity with God?" Tony said, "No, but I would be interested to hear how I could know." We set up a time that afternoon after he rested.

We met in Tony's hotel room, and I opened my Bible to show how he could have a personal relationship with God through Jesus Christ by confessing his sins and asking for the gift of eternal life that Jesus provided by his death on Calvary. It was like throwing a life jacket to a drowning man. I asked Tony to read Romans 10:9-10 from my Bible, "That if you confess with your mouth, 'Jesus is Lord,' and believe in your heart that God raised Him from the dead, you will be saved. For it is with your heart that you believe and are justified, and it is with your mouth that you confess and are saved." With brokenness, Tony confessed his sins and asked Jesus for the gift of eternal life.

The next day during treatment with 20 people listening in, Dan, another patient from Idaho who was an ordained minister, said, "Tony, I heard something happened to you yesterday afternoon" to which Tony replied, "Yeah I got saved and it was the greatest day of my life." Tony said he was not afraid of dying after that day. Tony was a roofer and he and his wife lived 50 miles outside Anchorage. They didn't have electricity or a phone, so I lost contact with Tony, but I am convinced I will see Tony Miller again when the Lord calls me to my eternal home.

My Lord has used cancer as a bridge to share with others, like Tony, who are going through cancer and don't have assurance of eternal life. The first was an English man who had spent time in Australia. A friend called me one Friday afternoon and told me he had tried to witness to a client of his named George who lived in San Francisco but my friend who had hearing deficiencies could not understand him well enough to present God's plan for eternal life. I called George, and we had a nice 20-minute visit about our cancer journey. I requested permission from George to ask him a couple of questions. When I asked him if he had received our Lord's gift of eternal life, George replied, "No, but I would like to know about that." I told George Moore the same truths I had shared with Tony Miller in California. George readily asked Jesus to forgive him his sins and asked him for the gift of eternal life. Later, I asked George if he knew where he would go if God called him home and he replied, "I would go to heaven." George also had a diagnosis of a life-threatening cancer with maybe three months to live. I sent George some literature about growing in his relationship with Jesus and how to tell others about Christ. I called George every three weeks, and we had great fellowship over the phone. The last time I spoke with George, he said, "Ken, I am at the hospital sharing with cancer patients about how they can receive the gift of eternal life." I never had the privilege of meeting George on this earth, but I firmly believe he will be one of the first to greet me when my Lord calls me home.

I never kept my cancer a secret. One day, I made a sales call on the purchasing manager of a good-sized company in Houston. He said, "Ken, I wish you could visit my mom. She has terminal cancer and is in Memorial Herman Southwest Hospital. Sara and I introduced ourselves to Mrs. Putnam and told her of her son's request that I visit her. Mrs. Putnam said she was afraid to die. I asked if she knew her eternal destination for sure and she said no. She was so ready to receive the good news of Jesus Christ's supreme sacrifice for man's sins and how

He died for her so she might receive the gift of eternal life. Mrs. Putnam eagerly asked Jesus to come into her life and told Sara she was not afraid to die anymore. A few weeks later her son also received the gift of eternal life.

If you are a true believer in Jesus and have cancer, God can use your story and cancer journey to share with those he will bring across your path how they can have peace with God and not be afraid of death. May God bless each of you as you travel this journey of life.

If you are reading this book and don't have the assurance that you are going to heaven when you die, you can stop right now and give your heart to Jesus.

Pray With Me

Lord Jesus, I believe You are God and that You died on the cross, were buried and raised again after three days for the forgiveness of my sins. I ask You to forgive me of my sins and come into my life to live. Thank You for Your gift of eternal life. In Jesus' name, amen.

Journal

Write your story about how you came to know Jesus personally. Learn to tell your story in just a few minutes so that you, like Ken, can lead others into the kingdom of God.

Verse to Memorize

> "For God so loved the world that He
> gave His one and only Son that whoever
> believes in Him shall not perish but have
> eternal life" (John 3:16)

Allyson's kept her soul strong by writing in her journal. When John found those nineteen journals, I read through them and pulled statements that touched my heart. Her journals were personal, poignant, and transparent. I won't share her actual prayers, but I know she would want you to read some of her statements.

Quotes From Allyson Stephens Journal

"People should be able to identify us not by what we have said about ourselves but how we live."

"My willingness to pursue what He wants rather than what I want is my love letter to Him."

"Each day I make a choice. I choose to be lazy; I choose to be average, or I choose to be excellent."

"Blessings are an expression of God's love for us coming at just the right time. Coming to us as a result of obedience."

જી

"I began day by day, giving it to God; not holding anything back and slowly, ever so slowly, God lifted me out of that pit."

જી

"Daily I must turn over the soil of my heart through repentance and confession."

જી

"God will not do through us what we don't allow Him to do to us."

જી

"Anything we manipulate to get, we will rarely keep."

❧

"We are to love with insight so we can love with compassion. We are never called to love blindly."

❧

"The intensity of my prayer should directly correlate to my situation."

❧

"Much of the time, difficult times push us away from prayer or keep it shallow because we don't want to get honest with how much we are really hurting."

❧

I take comfort in knowing it is not up to me to accomplish anything but just be willing to join His team."

❧

"Make your daily decisions in light of your destiny."

❧

"Living for God means I will stand out unsoiled; I will get a robe of white."

❧

"The more time I spend with John communicating, the more my desires become his and the more he desires to care for me."

❧

"Our marriage is a good reflection because it's healthy but even at that, it pales compared to the marriage I have with my Savior and Lord."

9

Mind Care

After a Stage 4 diagnosis, your mind goes crazy. All kinds of thoughts take up space in your head. Will I suffer and what will that look like? How long will I live and what will death feel like? How will my family make it if I am taken from them? Who will look after my parents? How do we get relief from all these thoughts that we have absolutely no control over? The Bible says in Romans 12:2 that we can be transformed by the renewing of our mind. But how does that happen? In this chapter, John and I will share how God renewed our minds with Scripture so that we could be the support our spouses needed during their Stage 4 journey.

God's Word is a weapon you will need to fight this gigantic battle of Stage 4. I know you don't feel you control these worrisome thoughts, but you do. 1 Corinthians 2:16 tells us, "For who has known the Lord's mind, that he may instruct Him? But we have the mind of Christ." If you are a Christian, you have the mind of Christ and the Holy Spirit lives inside of you. When these thoughts overwhelm us, the Bible tells us to take every thought captive to the obedience of Christ.

Two years before Shari was killed, God prepared me for what was to come. Scripture memory is a huge part of the First Place For Health program that I directed. One day my assistant, said, "Carole we have 100 memory verses in the program. Don't you think we should know all of them"?

In our program we memorize one verse each week and say it when we get on the scale to weigh. I, like so many of our members, would hurriedly learn the verse, say it in class and never think about it again. Pat , who hated exercise, challenged me, who loves exercise. If I would commit to learn those 100 verses, she would join me on the treadmills at church Monday through Friday, and we would learn one verse a week. This became our priority and after two years, we had committed 100 verses to memory by adding one new verse each week and practicing all the previous verses each day. We could say 100 verses in 30 minutes on the treadmill.

I tell you this story because when Shari died, those 100 Bible verses tucked deep into my heart saved my life. Those 100 verses kept me strong through our Stage 4 cancer journey and still help me today in my writing and speaking—and in my time with God each day.

I have chosen ten special verses and I encourage you to find this list in the back of this book and memorize the verses. When the lies from the enemy creep into your mind you will have an arsenal of truth from God's Word to use as your defense.

John said Scripture memory was also a part of his and Allyson's journey through Stage 4 cancer.

∞

After we moved to Katy, a church member who knew my family, knew my dad was a pastor for many years, knew that I grew up in church, and knew that I was teaching a couple's class at church, asked me to go to lunch. We had a wonderful visit, but he ended the gathering with an odd question directed at me, "How is your soul?" "My soul? I'm fine, my heart and my mind, all good. Why the question about my soul?"

He asked if we could meet again at his house for coffee the next week and I agreed. At his house, he prayed with me and asked if we could meet again the next week. We met every Wednesday morning for the next two years. Each week, he asked me to commit two verses of Scripture to memory (Navigators provide a structured series of verses). I discovered God was working through him to give me encouragement and a strength I would need on this cancer journey with my beautiful wife. I later discovered my soul was fine from the beginning of our coffee sessions, but my heart, mind, and soul were being protected with the Word I was having to commit to memory.

To this day, I recall Scripture when needed. I'm reminded how wonderful God is and that He loves me and cares for me and to lean on Him in the trials (which would be many). My favorite verse through this was a clear #1 for me. The first time I read it, I knew it was directed right at me.

"Do not be anxious about anything, but in everything, by prayer and petition, with thanksgiving, present your requests to God. And the peace of God, which transcends all understanding, will guard your hearts and your minds in Christ Jesus" (Philippians 4:6-7).

I recalled another verse after Allyson's memorial service when I went back to an empty house. "And let us consider how we may spur one another on toward love and good deeds, let us not give up meeting together, as some are in the habit of doing, but let us encourage one another—and all the more as we see the day approaching" (Hebrews 10:24-25). I was facing the unknown of living life without my best friend. We did everything together. My thoughts were centered on her, and I cherished the moments we had together. How would I move forward without having her by my side at night? What would dinners be like? During her illness, we drove to the country on the weekends, and Allyson found rest in the solitude of being alone at the ranch house. She didn't feel well enough to attend church the last year of her life, so we had our own quiet time together, reading scripture, praying, watching services on-line and TV which gave our hearts encouragement, but the gathering together with friends on Sunday morning was 12 months behind us. I suddenly realized that I needed encouragement and needed to get involved in a small group. The church (Christ followers) encourages others and being encouraged by others is central to the life of a believer in Christ. I am currently involved in a Thursday night Bible study and have plugged into a satellite branch of our former church. I so look forward to gathering with believers and being encouraged while seeking others who need to hear a word of encouragement as well.

My friend Mike Kelley reached out to me this week and sent a short message of encouragement ... including Psalm 121 in a brief text message. In times of uncertainty the words of the Psalmist are so encouraging, "I lift up my eyes to the mountains, where does my help come from? My help comes from the Lord, the Maker of heaven and earth ... The Lord will watch over your coming and going both now and forevermore." So comforting to read the words that He is watching over me now and forevermore. I am comforted knowing He is watching over me and knows my steps today and the days to follow.

Pray With Me

Dear Lord, the truth of Your Word calms our troubled minds. I pray that we will commit to memorize verses that will help transform our mind and help us to see that Your will is good, pleasing and perfect and to know that we will make it through this Stage 4 journey because You will be there every step of the way. In Jesus' name, amen.

Journal

Write about the thoughts you have been experiencing since your diagnosis. While many of these thoughts may torment you, all of them have a verse in the Bible that has the power to replace those troubling thoughts with God's truth.

Verse To Memorize

"Do not conform any longer to the
pattern of this world but be transformed
by the renewing of your mind. Then you
will be able to test and approve what
God's will is—His good, pleasing and
perfect will" (Romans 12:2).

ॐ

Allyson's Blog
Thankful for His Word

The words of the Lord Almighty hold power that we can't possibly comprehend. Over and over, I have witnessed this power released in my life's circumstances and each time I am taken back in such humility and also propelled forward in boldness. For the last several weeks, I have relied on the power of His Word to carry me through another round of physical uncertainties. It began with a paralyzed vocal nerve, which left me with a strained squeak for a voice and unrelenting back problems. Ongoing chronic pain has never been my cross to bear but I now have a deeper understanding of those who have had to maintain a positive outlook while having pain that never lets up. It is really hard. Life is always showing me that nothing on this side of heaven is certain but God and His presence with me during these uncertainties. With new and odd symptoms, my doctor ordered more than the usual tests. In a matter of weeks, I was told things are bad, things are good, things are not as good as we thought, actually things might be really good ... now we just don't know. That's pretty much word for word how it went. Because of the lack of clarity with the test results, the decision was made to stop all treatment for a few months and re-scan to see if my health is really good—or really not. Confused yet? This will give you a small glimpse into the window of my life recently. Physically, I have to accept a shade of grey. I actually found a definition in the thesaurus for a grey area. It is defined as an intermediate area; a place that is not clearly one thing or the other. BINGO, that would be me. Thankfully, because of high tech modern medicine, I have not had to deal with many seasons of not knowing and not having a clear plan as far as my cancer is concerned. No one I know likes not knowing or not having clear answers. None of us would choose to wait on these sorts of things. It is a big challenge for me, and I knew it could only be done with some sense of sanity by relying on the power of God's words. Coping with uncertainties by relying on the certainty of who God is and what He can do is my black and white.

The Holy Spirit has moved me to memorize and recall often Isaiah 51:15-16. You know I love to personalize scripture.

"I am the Lord your God, the One who churns the seas and causes the waves to roar." I love that He declared His greatness. When suddenly facing something fearful, I tend to make Him small mentally and unknowingly. He knows I do this, and He knew by redirecting me to His greatness, this would ground me, calm me, encourage me, and would sustain me in the weeks ahead. Not only does He highlight His power, but also He is personal.

When I am hit with a nerve-racking situation, I have a sense of urgency to get into His word and allow Him to remind me of how personal His power is to meet every need that will arise. I needed to see God is not any shade of grey, that He is an absolute and my future is clearly seen by Him.

"The Lord Almighty is My Name" It's as if He took His hands and cupped my face and said, "not only am I powerful, not only am I personal, but I am the Lord Almighty. Child, that is My Name. In any situation, this is always My Name. There is nothing I cannot do, and there is no uncertainty too uncertain for Me." For several days this one name for God became the super glue that kept my thoughts from scattering in a million different directions. If my thinking is not first influenced by who His is, I would go absolutely crazy.

"I put My words into your mouth." I first thought this somehow referred to my lack of vocal ability, but that lesson was too simple for God. He led me to see a much richer meaning in this verse. One morning I thought it would be wise to lay all of my test reports out on the table, along with the internet to help. I would study them carefully, not as patient, but as a nurse. This was not the brightest idea. An hour later, my mind was frustrated, angry, and anxious, to name a few emotions. I went straight to my Ipad to email a friend about all of my findings. Dumping all these negative emotions out only cleared the way for more negativity to rush back in. When I finished giving voice to each fear, I went back to correct my typos and before I clicked send, God clearly asked me, "Have I not put My words into your mouth? Have I not given you My promises to hold to?"

I replied, "Yes Lord, You have been so faithful to do that."

"These words coming out of your mouth are not Mine. These are yours."

Oh my, how conviction can make things crystal clear. All that He had been pouring into me is what He wants to spill out of me. His words spoken out loud have power for good, the power to change; they are positive based and seek to diminish rather than elevate fear and negativity as my words had done. His words leave the recipient blessed rather than drained. I backspaced every word until the negative novel I had written was deleted. Going forward, I have tried to be more cognizant of whose words I give voice to. He wants me to claim His words, and He certainly wanted no claim on mine.

"You are covered by the shadow of My right hand." Oh my goodness, how I needed to know about this shadow covering as I drove to so many appointments wondering what I would find out. It brought me a deep sense of peace that can't be explained any other way than His presence was with me. To remain in His shadow meant I needed to be intentional to walk close to Him. It gave me a visual of the closeness that He desires. To not allow myself to get so afraid that I lag or run ahead of God. Existing outside of His covering exposes me and makes me a easy target for the enemy of my soul. Fear has a way of pushing me outside of His protective covering, another reason there are so many verses telling me, "do not fear." "Have I not commanded you? Be strong and courageous. Do not be afraid; do not be discouraged, for the Lord your God will be with you wherever you go." I*n* Joshua 1:9, God assured Joshua He would go with him into battle, and He assures me daily He will go with me into mine.

"I am The One who set the heavens in their place and laid the foundations of the earth ... you are mine." With full authority, He reminds me, no one knows better how to minister to me than the One to whom I belong. When I was a child, no one knew better what my needs were than my mom. I trusted in that when I was young. As I grew into my teens, I questioned her many times, thinking I knew better. The same rings true in my relationship with God. Spiritually, He is the perfect parent, knowing every need before they arise, yet I struggle not to question and claim to know what is best for me. He leads me to a place of childlike faith, trusting completely that He knows better.

I hope by breaking down these two verses and sharing with you how God uses each word in my life will amaze you as it does me. When I started blogging, my intent was to bring glory to Him by sharing how He leads me to climb to that higher Rock (Psalm 61:2). That higher rock is always Himself. From this rock He provides a higher view, a place that is stable and secure, not uncertain or grey. This is what these two verses in Isaiah have done. I hope to encourage others to experience for themselves the power and clarity that is found when we exchange His words for our own.

~Allyson

10

Body Care

B ody care is important for everyone but especially for those whose bodies have been invaded by Stage 4. It doesn't matter if you have neglected your body your entire life or if you have taken good care of your body for years. Stage 4 is no respecter of persons because it attacks all kinds of people. You may be overweight, normal weight, or thin. You may be active or a couch potato. You may live in calm or have a nervous disposition. Perhaps you get the recommended eight hours of sleep, or you may be a fitful sleeper who only gets four to five hours. Those who are normal weight, exercise regularly, get enough rest, and manage their stress are the most surprised with the Stage 4 diagnosis while those who haven't taken care of their bodies aren't surprised and suffer from guilt that they neglected caring for their body.

Second Corinthians 4:16-17 says, "Therefore we do not lose heart. Though outwardly we are wasting away yet inwardly we are being renewed day by day. For our light and momentary troubles are achieving for us an eternal glory that far outweighs them all."

Our bodies are going to die, whether or not we have Stage 4. From the moment we take our first breath on earth, we are headed toward our last breath. As I've tried to share throughout this book, John and Allyson and Johnny and I lived with Stage 4 for many years, but we realized that Stage 4 was a beautiful gift. God used Stage 4 to change our lives radically, and except for the disease, it was changed for the better. We made changes in our priorities, relationships, marriage, and parenting that we might not have made without Stage 4.

As one who has studied and practiced a healthy lifestyle for almost forty years, I want you to understand that the key to healthy body care is moderation and consistency. Do what you can and trust God to sustain and prolong your life. God is the one who determines how long any of us will live. I hope you will take care of every area of your body, soul, mind, and spirit as you battle Stage 4. If you do, you will live in peace and joy in spite of this disease. As I write to you about the four areas of healthy body care, you will see that I am, most of all, practical. What you do must fit your lifestyle, and if you try to take better care of your body, God will move in with might and power and give you the desire and resources to do even more than you dreamed you could do. Rome wasn't built in a day so take several deep breaths and let's talk about body care.

There are four main areas of body care: good nutrition, exercise, sleep, and stress management.

Good Nutrition

Ken Lowrimore has practiced good nutrition since his diagnosis. I wanted to share part of his story here because Ken eats healthy.

> "When life throws you a lemon, give it to Jesus and let him make lemonade. My journey with cancer began while on a business trip to Clarence, New York (near Niagara Falls). I was on a week-long training trip to

a specialty battery manufacturer that made Lithium batteries. These batteries would operate up to 200 Deg. C. The training session began on Monday and was scheduled to end Friday. Midway thru the week, I experienced moderate-to-severe pain in my abdomen. The pain intensified, and I was concerned I might need to see a doctor in a strange city. God gave me strength to endure until I arrived home in Sugar Land, Texas.

I made an appointment with a doctor who diagnosed a viral infection and prescribed antibiotics. After taking the regimen of antibiotics, the pain increased, and I felt lethargic. I went back to the doctor, and he diagnosed an ulcer. When weeks of bland foods and medicine didn't alleviate the pain, he suggested I should see an oncologist.

Exploratory surgery, blood tests, CT scans, and a needle biopsy revealed I had NHL (non-Hodgkin's lymphoma) based on blood tests and CT scans. The biopsy discovered there were cancer cells in my bone marrow, which changed my diagnosis to Stage 4 NHL. I began chemo treatments.

In the meantime, I checked for alternative treatments and became convinced that good nutrition would go a long way in rebuilding my immune system, which the chemo had negatively impacted. I asked the doctor, "What is your estimation for my life expectancy with chemo?"

He said, "Two to five years?"

"What if I don't do any further chemo and instead do a regimen of nutrition that includes lots of raw fruits, vegetables, and raw nuts and carrot juice."

He said, "You will have a better quality of life with chemo and besides you can't cure NHL with nutrition."

"Doctor, I don't think I have much to lose, I'm going to try nutrition"

He said, "I don't need to see you until you decide to do your next chemo."

I continued to work for a year and felt well with the nutrition regimen. I had trouble breathing. A new oncologist told me I had an aggressive cancer growing in my tonsils. He began chemo immediately after a port was in place. With the strength my Lord Jesus gave me, I endured 52 hours of treatment and praise God, the swelling in my neck decreased and my breathing returned to normal. This time my body handled the chemo much better as I returned to work in a week and was never ill. I endured five more scheduled chemo treatments.

In the past 25 years, God has sustained me through 10 different chemo regimes, and I have memorized Nehemiah 8:10b, "The joy of the Lord is my strength."

❧

I am convinced, one reason Ken Lowrimore has lived twenty-five years with Stage 4 is that he changed his dietary intake at the beginning of his Stage 4 journey.

People go crazy when faced with Stage 4, especially in nutrition. We spent eleven days in Colorado Springs learning a vegan diet with daily organic coffee enemas and practiced this lifestyle for six months. I must be honest and say that I only practiced this lifestyle when we were together. At work, I ate the way I always had: healthy but including all the food groups. I stayed the same weight, but Johnny lost a lot of weight and looked really gaunt. It was hard and boring, everything was organic, with mostly raw fruits and vegetables. The only cooked food was a baked sweet potato once a day. Johnny finally said, "This is not living, and I'm not doing it." He still lived more than 16 years with Stage 4. God determines the number of our days, so trust Him to show you what to do and how to do it.

God created all food, but it is man who has adulterated most of it. Fast-food restaurants offer foods high in fat and sugar at a low price. There are some healthy offerings, but they are more expensive, so most people opt for the cheaper options because those are what they really desire. America faces an epidemic of obesity, which leads to diabetes, high blood pressure, and heart disease. Nutrition experts and medical professionals tell us that cancer feeds on sugar. Johnny was not a sugar eater and Allyson loved sugar, but neither of them was overweight. Moderation and consistency are the key to good body care.

In the First Place for Health program we eat from all the food groups, choosing good quality foods in the proper quantities. Our food plan is the same one that the USDA recommends, and you can find on Nutrition.gov. It is comprised of mostly whole grains, fruits, and vegetables, low in protein and fat with no added sugars. No food is forbidden but there are foods that should be eaten often and others, only occasionally or seldomly.

The Western diet is heavy on meat, but the FP4H food plan recommends six ounces of meat a day for most women and not much more than that for men. Most meat and dairy consumed today are full of growth hormones and antibiotics and contain saturated fat, the worst kind of fat. Meat and dairy are an area it might be wise to choose organic and range fed. Try to replace the amount of meat you eat with beans. Again, remember moderation and consistency.

In today's society there are so many diets and most of them eliminate one or more food groups. It is my belief that all the food groups are necessary to build strong cells to fight Stage 4, and I have developed different strategies for my personal lifestyle to get enough fruits and vegetables into my daily diet. I must be intentional if I want to eat two cups of vegetables each day and two cups of fruit, so here are two suggestions to make that happen. None of us became unhealthy or overweight from eating too many fruits and vegetables. We need a wide variety of fruits and vegetables because there are different vitamins and benefits found in all the different colors.

Yogurt Parfait

(I usually eat this for breakfast, so I get most of my fruit for the day)

¾ cup strawberries, diced   38 calories

¼ cup of blueberries   21 calories

½ banana   50 calories

Vanilla yogurt (I like Greek light) 80-100 calories

1/3 cup whole grain granola. 120 calories

1 ½ cups of fruit, 1 milk serving, and 1 grain serving and about 300 calories.

To get the number of vegetables I need each day (two cups), I make Mason jar salads. You can google these for all the different varieties, but the reason I make these is I am basically lazy and won't cut up or cook the vegetables

I need daily. I shop on Monday morning after I work out and make the 5 salads as soon as I get home. I save out enough salad to eat on Monday and have 5 left to eat the rest of the week. I use quart Mason jars with the wide mouth lid. The entire process takes less than an hour, and I am set for the week. Living alone, I usually eat out either lunch or dinner, so I eat the salad for the meal I am home.

Mason Jar Salad

¼ cup celery   4 calories

¼ cup bell Pepper   12 calories

¼ cup carrots   18 calories

¼ cup grape Tomatoes   10 calories

¼ cup cucumbers   11 calories

¼ cup mandarin oranges   40 calories

1 Tbsp craisins   25 calories

¼ cup feta cheese   70 calories

3 oz chicken breast (cooked, chopped)   165 calories

4 pitted Greek olives   40 calories

| 2 T Lite Vidalia Onion Dressing | 80 calories |

(I also love aged raspberry or lemon balsamic vinegar for my dressing; 0 calories)

| ¼ cup avocado | 95 calories |

(put avocado in when ready to serve)

| 2 cups raw spinach | 15 calories |

Total Calories   **585 calories**

2 cups vegetables, ½ cup fruit, 3 oz meat, 1 dairy, 2 fats

Layer ingredients starting with salad dressing on the bottom, tomatoes next, then layer putting spinach on top. Press spinach down, put on the lid. These jars of salad will stay crisp and fresh for a week. You can also add ¼ cup broccoli, ¼ cup cauliflower, and ¼ cup chopped onion. Lots of days I add one hard-boiled egg instead of the chicken. You can also add black beans or whole grain cooked pasta, quinoa, brown rice, or corn.

Adjust calorie count for any items you didn't consume.

Exercise

America is a sedentary nation with about 5 percent of our people exercising regularly. God designed our bodies to move, but since most of us no longer do hard physical labor as did our forefathers, we find it difficult to work regular exercise into our already busy schedule. I began regularly exercising the year before I turned forty and have exercised regularly for almost forty years. Before then, I never exercised at all and didn't play any sports growing up. I was thirty nine when FP4H began at my church and about that same time I ran into a friend at a shower who was my age and she looked great. I was never obese but usually needed to lose about twenty pounds. I had lost those twenty pounds many times, but always gained them back. I said to my friend, "how could you lose weight and not tell me?," to which she replied, "Carole, you know we are turning 40 next year. Do you want to be fat and forty?" Those words had a ring to them that sounded horrible, so I signed up immediately when the FP4H program was offered.

All these years of healthy eating and regular exercise have been good for me. I have excellent health and take no medicines. If you are reading this and have a diagnosis of Stage 4, I'm sure you are thinking, "This is unfair. I've done the same thing, and I have Stage 4." Eating healthy and exercising doesn't guarantee we won't be diagnosed with a life-threatening condition, but it does better our chances of being healthier than most people. People who eat healthy foods and exercise have a stronger immune system than those who don't. I am 79 and this body is going to wear out at some point. My goal is to continue walking upright as long as possible.

Both Johnny and Allyson always had an active lifestyle. Johnny played football, basketball, and baseball in high school, and Allyson was a cheerleader. Early in our marriage Johnny played on an amateur baseball team and after our son, John, was old enough, Johnny coached his football, basketball, and baseball teams until he started playing sports in middle school. Johnny never exercised like me, but he stayed active.

After his Stage 4 diagnosis, I encouraged him to exercise with me, but his usual reply was, "I'm going to start on Monday." He exercised sporadically on a mini trampoline or on the treadmill at home, but never on a regular basis.

Allyson loved to walk, and she walked almost every day in her neighborhood. I thought because she had always been thin that she also ate only healthy foods but found out differently when I stayed in her home. Allyson was naturally thin and stayed that way because she was always busy and didn't overeat. Remember, moderation and consistency are the key.

The most important reason someone with a Stage 4 diagnosis needs a regular exercise routine is it will keep your bones and immune system strong as you go through treatment. Regular exercise will also elevate your mood if you struggle with depression.

In FP4H, we recommend two to three days of strength training/core work and two to three days of aerobic exercise like walking every week. These can be combined or stretched out over the week. It is wise to strength train every other day, but you can walk every day if you desire. I began a strength training program twelve years ago when I was sixty-seven, and it has been a big plus as I age. I began using three to five lb. weights and now use fifteen to twenty-five lb. weights. I love my functional strength. I can carry six bags of groceries in at once or lift and carry 24 bottles of water into the house. Muscle strength declines between 16-40 percent after age forty. The good news is that muscle can be built back with strength training.

In FP4H we say, "If you can barely walk, then start barely walking" and "something is better than nothing and more is better than less." I have an Apple watch which is a great motivator for me because I like to close the exercise rings each day. I also have friends with Apple watches, and we hold each other accountable because we see when a friend closes all their rings. I used a FitBit for years and that's also a great tool to see that you are getting enough steps each day; 10,000 steps a day are recommended for good health. There are many free apps available for both strength training and aerobic exercise. Just begin and your body will thank you. These can be done at home with minimal equipment, so don't think you have to join a gym or hire a trainer to exercise. Remember, moderation and consistency are the key.

Rest

Our bodies need rest and quality sleep every day. Seven to eight hours of sleep each night is recommended for adults and even more hours for children. Many people get much less. Our body repairs and heals while we sleep. Those with Stage 4 will most likely need added rest periods during the day while on treatment.

Stress Management

We live in a stress-filled world. Watching people's anxiety and fear during the Covid-19 pandemic made me sad. I have learned to deal with stress, so trials or pandemics do not cause me anxiety or fear. When you receive a Stage 4 diagnosis, you may find it hard to manage stress. You play the tape to the end in your mind and get the wrong message because the tape always ends in your mind with a soon-coming death. As you learn to live with your diagnosis, you will start thanking God for each day and each blessing in that day. Thankfulness is a huge deterrent to living a stress-filled life.

I asked John to share about fear versus faith in his and Allyson's journey.

⋰⋱

John's Words on Fear or Faith

Allyson and I were hurting when we received the Stage 4 diagnosis, but we had another 24 years of blessedness. I want to let you know that the fears we had that day were not warranted. If God had cut a deal with us that he would grant us another 20 years together with little or no interruption, we would have gladly taken it. We trusted him fully. We agreed not to walk with our head down and allow fear to take over our home. Instead, we read his Word and trusted that he was in control of all things big and small. Allyson would tell me often that she was comforted in knowing how much He loved her, and she would walk in faith and trust Him regardless of the outcome. She wanted to stay here with us—she loved her life—but she also wanted to trust Him fully even in death. The story below about trusting God in the lowest moments speaks about our meeting in the driveway and her telling me that she was Stage 4.

Fighting back the tears with her head pressed against me, she said she wanted to live long enough so the boys would know how much she loved them and if God would grant her that much time on this earth, her prayer would be answered. We had 24 more years; the boys knew how much she loved them. We would sometimes laugh about her prayer; she didn't have enough faith to ask for enough time on this earth so that the grandkids would know how much she loved them. We were so blessed, and our prayer was answered. The boys are doing great. Their path was paved with many prayers from Allyson, and they are walking examples of her powerful prayer life. I am a better person because seeing her faith journey allowed me to grow even deeper in my faith walk. Even after her passing, I am changing because of what she instilled in me. I believe her kindness and compassion was passed on to me. I have become a lot more aware of my surroundings, and I seek those who need a word of encouragement. It is not how

I am wired. I am not someone to slow down and notice those who might be hurting or needing an encouraging word. I have always been aloof to my surroundings or insensitive to those who are struggling with a trial. Even during Allyson's diagnosis, I was not very tender with the boys or even Allyson at times. I am not a very sensitive or very compassionate person, but now I look for the opportunity to bless others more than ever. Maybe she left something behind for me to carry on. I'm not sure if the change in me directly results from watching and learning from her or maybe it's the many prayers being spoken for me. I just know I'm a better person and I am enjoying helping others more than ever before.

One day, I met her in the driveway after work after a doctor's appointment. It was her usual checkup, but this time it was not usual. Dr. Cagle told her the cancer was Stage 4, and she had a 50/50 chance of surviving another six months. I was stunned by the news. I didn't know how to respond, much less what to say. She was in tears. I hurt for her and thought about the future and what it might look like without her in it ... what is life going to be like when she is gone? I didn't see life playing out this way. I thought we would live a long time together and walk through life just the way I visualized it. We were supposed to grow old together.

Allyson made it six months. She made it six years. She lived another 24 years, and our lifestyle didn't change much. If anything changed, it was our faith. Our faith grew, and our love for each other grew. Our life together was so much more precious. Every moment from that day forward was not taken for granted. Now, 25 years after that devastating news in the driveway in front of our house, I am living this life alone and trusting God will lead me to new beginnings. I don't know what lies ahead, but I am not concerned with the unknown or what may be around the corner. I walk with a childlike faith, not knowing what tomorrow may bring, but whatever he chooses for me I am willing. The ability to hold my head up with confidence and walk thru this next chapter of life with confidence was met with a moment that I've shared with just a few people.

That dreadful news that she shared with me in the driveway of our home was a moment in time that I will never forget, it was a low moment for the both of us—it's a moment I can visualize and recall easily—clearly as if it happened yesterday. But I had another stand still moment a few days later. I don't remember exactly how many days had passed, but it was maybe 3 or 4 days later. I was hurting for her and dreading what life might be like if she were not around. We lived in Conroe, Texas. My work was on the west side of Houston. For ten years I had been driving fifty-five miles to work and many times I would leave our home while our two boys (ages two and five) were still asleep and many nights I arrived home after they were already in bed. How could I balance work and home life as a single parent? How could I stay strong and continue to manage at work knowing what was in the future? I hate to admit it, but I was thinking she would not make it, and I was going to have to decide how to find a caretaker to commit to being at the house for ten to twelve hours a day. And I thought it would be foolish for me to continue working such long hours and not be home with the boys after they lost their mother. A short time later, I was driving to work and had turned off of I-45 heading west on Beltway 8 and praying out loud. My voice was breaking. I was trying to be strong, but I was broken, and I needed something more. I needed strength that was not present, and I was tired of fighting the emotions on my own. Yes, I was praying with her and I was prayerful when alone, but on this day, I was broken. I felt anxiety creep in. I was tired of facing the what ifs and allowing fear to take hold of my heart and mind. I left the prayerful tone and the somewhat scripted prayer and just started speaking to the Lord as if He was beside me. My conversation was no longer about saying what seemed spiritual; it was real as I poured out my heart and all the fears that were lingering and all the doubts that were creeping in were being sent directly to Him. I pleaded for His mercy and grace. "God I need you now. Speak clearly and open my mind." It was a moment I will always remember because I changed from that moment forward. I heard a still small voice say, "Do you trust me?" I remember thinking, 'Now we are getting somewhere. We are having a conversation and it feels like You are right here with me. The answer is yes, I trust You.

He said, "You trust Me with the smaller things, but do you think I'm big enough to handle all things large and small?" I was caught off guard. I realized I did trust Him in the smaller things, I trusted Him to meet our needs, and I trusted Him to guide our path. I was confident that He loved me enough to sustain me when it wasn't too bad, but this circumstance seemed bigger than God Himself. And in my heart, I felt the Spirit comfort me, "I'm big enough to handle every trial or circumstance you face. Trust Me." From that day forward, I have walked with much faith, and I can recall those words that were spoken to me that day.

The Lord spoke in a still small voice. It was just what I needed, a still small voice. It still rings true today. I trust Him with all things. Even 24 years later, Allyson trusted Him with her life. One of her last requests to me and the boys was to let everybody know God is faithful. Even in those last few days, knowing how it was going to end when hospice stepped in daily administering the right amount of medication and telling us it wouldn't be long, she whispered to her family, "He is faithful."

The calming voice and presence of the Lord is not found in the noise; it is found in the quiet. The Lord speaks to us in a low whisper, but the problem is we don't hear His voice because our ears are not tuned toward heaven. Too often, we are focused on the earthly things. We can hear the voice of the Lord best when we are quiet. We need to step away from the wind, earthquakes, and fires of this world and prepare our hearts to receive a word from the Lord. Seek Him in prayer, but remember to be still and listen. Quiet your heart and open your ears to hear the still, small voice of God. You may be in the middle of some terrible situation, but the low whisper is coming.

Pray With Me

Dear Lord, I know that this body I live in belongs to You. I am asking You to show me how to take better care of my body. Help me eat healthy foods, exercise my body, get enough rest, and not fear what the future holds. Stay close to me, I pray. In Jesus' name, amen.

Journal

Write specific steps you want to take to take better care of your body in the areas of nutrition, exercise, rest, and stress management.

Verse To Memorize

"Therefore we do not lose heart. Though outwardly we are wasting away yet inwardly we are being renewed day by day. For our light and momentary troubles are achieving for us an eternal glory that far outweighs them all"
(2 Corinthians 4:16-17).

Allyson's Blog
Resist or Submit

This month God has had me thinking more about His desire to be my Lord. For Him to lead and me to follow. Becoming a Christian meant I became a follower of Jesus who said in John 14:6 "I am the way and the truth and the life." However, the decision to follow didn't stop there, it began there. More and more He has layered to my knowledge of what it looks like to daily follow Him. I say with my words that I want to follow His lead, yet my inner self is always fighting to take the posture of resistance more often than submission. It's not a bold "my way or the highway" attitude, but a more subtle and sneaky attitude that creeps in, and I don't even realize that I am resisting Him. If I'm being honest and we examined my words and my thoughts this month, I have resisted to trust. I have resisted to believe a promise He has given me. I resisted waiting on Him to act on my behalf and resolved to solve the issue myself. I have resisted obeying when it challenged what I wanted or didn't want to do. I resist hope especially when my prayers seem to go unnoticed. Sometimes I have even resisted His forgiveness. These are just a few honest examples. I see spiritual resistance on my part is an opposing force that seeks to restrain me from walking in the freedom that comes when I submit. The word *submission* or *surrender* implies to yield to the authority of another and for a lot of us provokes thoughts of losing our rights or freedom, but in the spiritual sense the opposite is true. It is when I stop resisting and surrender fully to trust His lead, then I am free to believe, "He's got this."

Knowing that He desires me to live under His Lordship is much more than just surrendering when I feel I am losing a battle or my back is against the wall, and there is nothing left I can do to help myself. It starts with an honest look at my posture right now before I feel my back is against the wall.

Lately I had been walking our old dog and my son's new dog together. There is a huge difference in their walking posture. My old lab heels on my left side following my lead because we've had nearly twelve years of walking experience together, and he has no problem surrendering the lead to me. The puppy on the other hand has very little walking experience. She pulls far out in front as the leash will allow, straining against my leading. She isn't gaining anything by straining so hard to be out in front except distance from me.

In my relationship with God, sometimes I'm like an inexperienced puppy. I utilize my energy to strain to find the answers I think I need or to fix all the problems I think I have—rather than simply sticking close to my Lord and submitting to His leading. I invite a distance to set in between me and God.

Priscilla Shirer wrote this in her study, *Discerning the Voice of God*, "God is not as much interested in us reaching our destination as He is in the knowledge of Him we gain while we are on the journey." I had to read that statement a few times through to let it sink in, but how true this is. Sometimes I position myself so far out in front that I miss the blessing He has for me in the walk.

His word tells us in James 1:2 that we will have trials of many kinds to walk through yet when they come my initial posture is like something from the movie Karate Kid. I go into full resistance mode rather than trusting what He leads me to, He will lead me through.

When I made my decision to follow Christ public so many years ago, the song the church sang that day was "I Surrender All." I am thankful God left this in my mind to recall because every time I hear it I remember what my hearts desire was then and what I want it to be now—a heart that sticks close to my Lord.

~ Allyson

All to Jesus I surrender;
all to him I freely give;
I will ever love and trust him,
in his presence daily live.

I surrender all, I surrender all,
all to thee, my blessed Savior,
I surrender all.

All to Jesus I surrender;
humbly at his feet I bow,
worldly pleasures all forsaken;
take me, Jesus, take me now.

I surrender all, I surrender all,
all to thee, my blessed Savior,
I surrender all.

All to Jesus I surrender;
make me, Savior, wholly thine;
fill me with thy love and power;
truly know that thou art mine.

I surrender all, I surrender all,
all to thee, my blessed Savior,
I surrender all.

All to Jesus I surrender;
Lord, I give myself to thee;
fill me with thy love and power;
let thy blessing fall on me.

I surrender all, I surrender all,
all to thee, my blessed Savior,
I surrender all.

All to Jesus I surrender;
now I feel the sacred flame.
O the joy of full salvation!
Glory, glory, to his name![1]

1   Judson W. Van de Venter (1855-1939). Public Domain

11

To Live Is Christ

One morning, while riding the bike at John and Allyson's beautiful fitness center, I was listening to a podcast of Chuck Swindoll speaking on "Laughing Through the Dilemmas of Life." He referenced Philippians 1:21, where Paul says, "For to me, to live is Christ and to die is gain." As I was riding the stationary bike and listening to the podcast, I felt the Holy Spirit was telling me to write what the Lord had been showing me during the three weeks I had been with Allyson and John.

What does "to live is Christ" mean? In Allyson's life it meant she and John modeled for their boys what the

Christian life is about. John taught them how to be men, but Allyson taught them so much through her journey with cancer. Her boys called or texted her every day. They loved to come or just visit on the phone. One week, flowers arrived from Tyler and his wife, Hannah. The boys are who they are today because of her cancer, not in spite of it. Allyson modeled grace and trust in Christ every step of the way, so her boys knew God would carry them through whatever life brings as well. John learned so much about servant leadership as he loved and served Allyson during this journey. Truly, for them to live is Christ.

Allyson's last two years were difficult, with lots of pain as the cancer spread. She had been both mad and sad that she might not live to see Tyler and Hannah's two little girls grow up. Allyson also wanted to see Ben married and have a family. However, she believed God gave her what she had asked for—raising her boys to adulthood. She had God's peace in the middle of cancer, and it never left her. Because of Allyson's life and witness, she had a hoard of friends fighting over who would get to take care of her every need. I watched them call, text, and bring food and gifts the entire time I was there.

After listening to the message by Chuck Swindoll, I also pondered what Paul meant when he wrote "to die is gain." A few years ago, I lost a dear friend named Jennifer Kennedy Dean, who died suddenly of a heart attack. She had not been sick, so I have tried to process Paul's words. Jennifer wrote twenty-five books on prayer. Her life will live on much like Oswald Chambers because of the depth of her writing and speaking. I have prayed and asked God to not let me miss what He still has for me to do. Time is short for all of us. Somehow, it seems shorter when a friend has cancer, but unless the Lord Jesus comes back to get us, we are all going to die.

I will continue pondering what Paul meant, but I believe when the Lord Jesus calls me home, my work on this earth will be done. Death doesn't mean it's over. I may do more in death than I did in life. If I have lived Philippians 1:21 as Paul said, "to live is Christ" then my death will be "gain" in so many ways. My family and friends will know that they must carry on the legacy I left for them. The best part is that I will be with the Lord forever, free of pain or disease, the bonds of old age broken. I will see my loved ones again who have gone on before and the ones left behind who know Jesus. I have no doubt that because of Allyson Bell Stephens's life and death, her husband John and boys, Tyler and Ben, will lift the torch higher and that they will know fully that "to live is Christ and to die is gain."

I asked John to share with me how he and the boys are doing now. He wrote about what an encourager Allyson was and how it has left a legacy for their family.

Be Encouraged

You must decide that you are going to move on. It won't happen automatically. You will have to rise up and say,

"I don't care how hard this is. I don't care how disappointed I am. I'm not going to let this get the best of me. I'm moving on with my life." ~Joel Osteen

As I was driving home this evening, I was listening to one of the news channels on XM Radio. A guest mentioned PTG, and it caught my attention. I had never heard this term, but it stuck with me. I could relate to the idea of coming out stronger on the other side. I don't know how losing Allyson and my dad in the same month might have affected my well-being. I know it left a void, and I was hurt by the loss. But I didn't allow it to keep me down. I decided long ago that my relationship with Christ would sustain me and carry me through any challenges or adversity that might come my way. He has proven faithful so many times before, and whatever would be viewed as tragic, I decided it would be an opportunity for growing my faith even deeper.

Post-traumatic growth (PTG) is a theory that explains this kind of transformation following trauma. It was developed by psychologists in the mid-1990's. People who endure psychological struggle following adversity can often see positive growth afterward. In layman's terms, experiencing adversity has its benefits, driving the individual to a higher level of functioning. I have heard the term PTSD (post traumatic stress disorder) many times, but I had never heard the term post-traumatic growth.

Losing someone close to you is a traumatic experience, and it's never easy to lose loved ones as their memories linger. It's been almost two years now; I think about Allyson every day, but many times I smile as I know she would enjoy the moment or appreciate some particular experience. The memory of her is not always a moment of sadness. I often remember our life together and how grateful I was to have had her near me as long as I did. My strength is returning, my confidence continues to grow, and I'm encouraged with each passing day. Life keeps going. It doesn't slow down. I have more responsibility as I am now filling both her role and mine. So I ask myself, "What is giving me the strength to move forward? How am I encouraged as I navigate life, yet she's not in it?" I knew that my relationship with Jesus Christ would sustain me, but I didn't expect to be as content as I am without her walking beside me.

I have been purposeful in my actions, and I have continued to stay close to friends and family, seldom turning down the opportunity to congregate and fellowship when invited to do so. I committed to memory Hebrews 10:24-25, and I've used it often when visiting with others who were hurting: "And let us consider how we may spur one another on toward love and good deeds, Let us not give up meeting together, as some are in the habit of doing, but let us encourage one another— and all the more as you see the day approaching." This is a great message to all of us, it calls us to be encouragers to one another.

The word "encourage" in Greek is parakaleo. Para *means alongside, and* kaleo *means to call, to beckon, or to speak to someone. When these two words are combined, the new word depicts someone who comes right alongside a person, urging him on.*

In the ancient Greek world, this word was often used by military leaders before sending troops into battle. Rather than hiding from the reality of war, the leaders gathered the troops and spoke about the potential dangers of the battlefield and then encouraged the troops by reminding what victory looks like. I have noticed that I am encouraged when I share how God has sustained me and carried me. It is encouraging each time I share my story, and it equally benefits the listener, as I am a walking testament of his goodness. When reflecting on the richness of the Greek word parakaleo, *I've listed a few examples.*

- *A coach giving a half-time speech to his team that is beaten down, reminding them of the game plan and how it will prevail—and if each player does their part, they will come out victorious.*

- *A parent picking up a frightened child crying out for comfort and reassuring that it is going to be all right.*

- *A physician who gives the news to one of their patients that it is going to be all right; the surgery went well; you are on the road to recovery.*

- *A military officer who summons up the troops and calmly encourages the frightened soldiers, "Together we will overcome and see victory."*

- *A defense attorney pleading the case for his client, making an appeal before the judge.*

Allyson was an encourager. She fully understood the visual of bringing life to someone who was hurting. Much like the child crying out, she would be the comforter for the situation.

As a nurse, she cherished the moment she could heal a wound, whether it was physical or mental. She loved to bring healing to others who were hurting. When our boys were navigating the challenges of life, Allyson wrote notes or she sent texts or handwritten letters. She put what they needed to hear in written form so they could hear what she had to say at a time they were willing to hear it. They kept the notes in their drawers and did not throw them away. From time to time, when I'm looking for batteries or some book, I'll unfold a note tucked deep inside a drawer and read her written words that still resonate. The boys and I always appreciated her written notes. They were always on point and written in such a way that they left no room for error. She was always right. My work requires a lot of travel and many times I found a written note meant to encourage me. She wrote how much she valued my character and the examples I was setting for others. She reminded me how much she loved our relationship and valued our time together and couldn't wait for me to return home. Sometimes she shared her deepest thoughts relative to what God was showing her and wanted me to be in a still quiet place where I could take the time to ponder on it too. She'd ask me to join her in a prayer request. I am guilty of moving at the speed of business, so instead of typing an email or taking the time to write a personal note, I preferred to say it—so I can move on to the next agenda item on my busy lists. Allyson demonstrated her thoughts in *writing because her heart wanted to make sure her words were heard and heartfelt at the same time. It takes time to be an encourager. Time to reflect and pen your words and make sure you are stating what that person needs to hear.*

To be an encourager, you have to be right with God, and your heart has to be in the right place if you want to be Spirit-led. I would attribute her ability to bring about a change in attitude for so many people to be directly tied to her morning quiet times that equipped her to be our moral compass of the home. She dedicated a special place in our home where she would retreat to for a moment of quiet solitude with her notebook in hand, a pen and yellow highlighter, some devotional books, and her Bible. It's a small nook on her side of the closet (our closet is huge, so don't let the visual of her in a closet be of concern). It is big enough to drop a beanbag chair and a side table large enough to hold a lamp, a cup of coffee, and all her books with room to spare. She loved that area of the home and when friends would visit, she liked showing them her study in that small nook tucked away in her corner of the closet. It was her place to get away from the hustle and find quiet solitude. She spoke her heart, but more importantly listened quietly to whatever word the Lord wanted to share with her that morning. This quiet time was an everyday occurrence that was started as soon as the boys were out the door. She made a cup of coffee, spent time in prayer, and took a long walk at the end. It was her routine as long as I can remember. By noon, she was in the best spirit and ready to take on whatever life would throw at her. She set her heart on encouragement and to be the one sending a word of encouragement to whoever needed it that day.

ॐ

I love the story of my friend, Catherine Cutrell Peake. Catherine has lived with Stage 4 for twelve years and her life is one of encouragement to all who know her. Even though her cancer recently returned in her kidney she has a vibrancy and zest for living that is contagious to all who know her.

Catherine Cutrell Peake

When I was 35 years old, a lump popped up on my right breast. The radiologist said, "Unfortunately, I do not have good news for you. I am 99.9 percent sure you have breast cancer." I had a 3-year-old little boy and a 6-month-old baby girl, and I was completely devastated. After many tests and scans, I learned the breast cancer had spread to my liver, my lung, in my left shoulder bones, and two lymph nodes—Stage 4.

Christmas came at the end of my six months of heavy chemo—our baby girl's first Christmas. I thought, *Is this my last Christmas?* or *Will I be bald at Carrington's first Christmas?* And then I thought, *Girl, you just need to get over yourself and out of this crazy pity party because once it starts it snowballs into craziness.*

After the heavy chemo, they could not find any cancer in me. I believe God used that chemo, and He healed me like he promised. But a board of doctors decided to do a radical, single mastectomy and remove 28 lymph nodes followed with about six weeks of radiation.

After other complications and a hysterectomy, it was clear I would be on chemo for the rest of my life. My pet scans have been coming back stable and I thank God for his mercy.

In the Message Bible, 2 Corinthians 12:7-8 says,

"Because of the extravagance of those revelations, and so I wouldn't get a big head, I was given the gift of a handicap to keep me in constant touch with my limitations. Satan's angel did his best to get me down; what he in fact did was push me to my knees. No danger then of walking around high and mighty! At first I didn't think of it as a gift, and begged God to remove it. Three times I did that, and then he told me, My Grace is enough; it's all you need. My strength comes into its own in your weakness."

I quit focusing on the handicap of Stage 4 and began appreciating the gift. Christ's strength moving in on my weakness. Now I take limitations in stride, and with good cheer, these limitations that cut me down to size—abuse, accidents, opposition, bad breaks. I just let Christ take over. And so the weaker I get, the stronger I become.

After eleven years of being NED (no evidence of disease) my urologist found some cancer lesions in my kidney. I fell apart until I remembered my hope lies in my Abba, my heavenly father, who still has great plans for me. He has the story he has written just for me all planned out, and I am so thankful that He is and will take care of every detail just the way He has planned it!

❧

I promise not only will you learn to live with Stage 4 but you will experience God's grace like all the people in this book have experienced it. Our Lord will help you and teach you truths you never dreamed possible. Trust Him as you learn "to live is Christ."

❧

Pray With Me

Dear Lord, Our prayer as we have read this book is that we will come through this experience with a greater knowledge of how much You love us and how much You care. Take care of us as we make this journey with You. In Jesus' name, amen.

Journal

Write about where you are right now. If you have found encouragement, write about what you want to do during this time? If you are still afraid and anxious, read the book again and begin memorizing the verses from each chapter. You will get stronger as time goes by.

Verse To Memorize

"For I know the plans I have for you," declares the Lord, "plans to prosper you and not to harm you, plans to give you hope and a future" (Jeremiah 29:11).

Allyson's Blog
A Victor in the Midst

Recently, I have felt like God has wanted me to focus on and write about victory. As I put the period at the end of that sentence, I realize it is because I need it. I've been in an attitude slump. The last couple of weeks were difficult for various reasons, not just for me but for others I love and care about as well. It just seems like there is one new concern after another.

When the trials multiply, it's hard to muster up the word *victorious* in my vocabulary. I know it is not just a word He wants me to have in my vocabulary, but an attitude He wants me to have as I walk through challenging days. I also know words don't have any benefit in my life if they don't affect my attitude.

Others may not see it, but I know when my attitude is "off" and I know God knows as well. I zeroed in on 1 John 5:4-5 where it says, "for everyone born of God overcomes the world, even our faith. Who is it that overcomes? Only he who believes that Jesus is the Son of God". A very simple emphatic statement of great value when applied to any present-day circumstance.

Since age eleven I have confessed my belief that Jesus is the only Son of God and have accepted what He did for me at the cross; therefore God tells me simply and clearly there has not been a moment since that time nor will there be a moment going forward where I don't stand victorious. *Who is it that has the victory? Who is it that overcomes? It is you, Allyson.* Despite how many concerns I see, despite what I feel, despite my doubts, it is a truth I must know, and that truth should be impacting my attitude.

In the fourth stanza of "Joyful, Joyful, We Adore Thee," Henry van Dyke wrote, "Ever singing march we onward, Victors in the midst of strife..." He didn't write victors when we conquer strife but victors in the midst of strife. If we conquer something, we feel a sense of winning, but God never intended for victorious living to be about a feeling of conquering or winning. It goes much deeper.

When asked to speak about living with cancer, I am very careful not to make the cancer my enemy and state. I will conquer my disease because the reality is I may not conquer it on this side of heaven. My daily battle is with my attitude and perspective of how I choose to view what God has allowed in my life. This applies not just to my cancer, but for every situation that burdens me.

For years I was in a Bible study and one phrase left a forever impression on me was take the higher view of God. When life hands me more challenges and more concerns, as it has recently, it is easy to feel like I'm losing rather than gaining. My view the last few days has been one of looking outward at all the stuff that concerns me, rather than looking up and soaking up a better view. A view of The Mighty One, God, The Lord, who speaks and summons the earth from the rising of the sun to where it sets (Psalm 50:1). A view of Jesus my Savior sitting at His right side interceding on my behalf. (Romans 8:34). This is the view I must keep if I am going to be a victor in the midst of strife.

Referring to this classic hymn, I can see two ways to turn my sights up and gain back a victorious attitude. I am to continue praising and to continue marching. I am to press on.

Anyone who has played a game with me knows if I feel I am losing in a game, I lose interest and would prefer to quit—but this is not an attitude I can apply to life. We are admonished to continue on. In 1 Corinthians 15 after speaking about our perishable bodies one day becoming imperishable (Praise God for this promise!) in verse 57 Paul says,"But thanks be to God! He gives us the victory through our Lord Jesus Christ."

Our victory is not in the absence of struggles or in an outcome we are praying for, but in a person, and when I choose to hold on to this truth, I hold on to a person. I won't quit praying for the outcomes I hope to see, but I need to remember to try to not equate those outcomes with the victory that is already mine in the person of Jesus Christ - in whom I can always rejoice and always have hope. Only then will my attitude truly reflect whether I am looking outward at the things or looking up at a person who is "capable of doing immeasurably more than I could ever ask or imagine" (Ephesians 3:20)

~Allyson

"My grace is sufficient for you, my power is made perfect in weakness" (2 Corinthians 12:9).

Addendum

Helpful Bible Verses to Read and Memorize

A spiral index that contains 50 cards is a great tool to keep these verses close. Memorizing a verse each week will be life changing and will give you a weapon to use to combat worry, fear, and depression. As you add another verse each week, continue practicing the verses you have already learned. Your life will become hope filled instead of hopeless.

Listed first are the eleven memory verses from each chapter. After that are some more helpful verses to give you hope and encouragement.

Chapter 1 Memory Verse

"May the God of hope fill you with all joy and peace as you trust in Him so that you may overflow with hope by the power of the Holy Spirit." Romans 15:13

Chapter 2 Memory Verse

"I would have despaired if I had not believed I would see the goodness of the Lord in the land of the living." Psalm 27:13

Chapter 3 Memory Verse

"Whether you turn to the right or to the left, your ears will hear a voice behind you, saying, 'This is the way; walk in it.'" Isaiah 30:21

Chapter 4 Memory Verse

"Trust in the Lord with all your heart and lean not on your own understanding; in all your ways acknowledge Him and He will make your paths straight." Proverbs 3:5-6

Chapter 5 Memory Verse

"Do not be anxious about anything, but in everything, by prayer and petition, with thanksgiving, present your requests to God. And the peace of God, which transcends all understanding, will guard your hearts and your minds in Christ Jesus." Philippians 4:6-7

Chapter 6 Memory Verse

"Do not store up for yourselves treasures on earth, where

moth and rust destroy, and where thieves break through and steal. But store up for yourselves treasures in heaven, where moth and rust do not destroy and where thieves do not break in and steal. For where your treasure is, there will your heart be also." Matthew 6:19-21

Chapter 7 Memory Verse

"The Lord does not look at the things man looks at. Man looks at the outward appearance, but the Lord looks at the heart." 1 Samuel 16:7b

Chapter 8 Memory Verse

"For God so loved the world that He gave his one and only Son, that whoever believes in Him shall not perish but have eternal life." John 3:16

Chapter 9 Memory Verse

"Do not conform any longer to the pattern of this world, but be transformed by the renewing of your mind. Then you will be able to test and approve what God's will is— His good, pleasing and perfect will." Romans 12:2

Chapter 10 Memory Verse

"Therefore we do not lose heart. Though outwardly we are wasting away, yet inwardly we are being renewed day by day. For our light and momentary troubles are achieving for us an eternal glory that outweighs them all." 2 Corinthians 4:16-17

Chapter 11 Memory Verse

"'For I know the plans I have for you,'" declares the Lord, 'plans to prosper you and not to harm you, plans to give you hope and a future.'" Jeremiah 29:11

༅

More Helpful Verses

"Yet this I call to mind and therefore I hope: Because of the Lord's great love we are not consumed, for His compassions never fail. They are new every morning; great is your faithfulness." Lamentations 3:21-23

༅

"We continually remember before our God and Father your work produced by faith, your labor prompted by love, and your endurance inspired by hope in our Lord Jesus Christ." 1 Thessalonians 1:3

"I am the light of the world. Whoever follows me will never walk in darkness, but will have the light of life." John 8:12

"Your Word is a lamp to my feet and a light for my path." Psalm. 119:105

"Who among you fears the Lord and obeys the word of his servant? Let him who walks in the dark, who has no light, trust in the name of the Lord and rely on his God." Isaiah 50:10.

"I will be glad and rejoice in your love, for you saw my affliction and knew the anguish of my soul." Psalm. 31:7

"I love the Lord because he hears my voice and my prayer for mercy. Because he bends down to listen, I will pray as long as I have breath! Death wrapped its ropes around me; the terrors of the grave overtook me. I saw only trouble and sorrow. Then I called on the name of the lord: 'Please, Lord save me!' How kind the Lord is! How good he is! So merciful, this God of ours!" Psalm 116:1-5 NLT

"Be joyful always, pray continually, give thanks in all circumstances, for this is God's will for you in Christ Jesus." 1 Thessalonians 5:16-18

"For my thoughts are not your thoughts, neither are my ways your ways," declares the Lord." Isaiah 55:8

❧

"Consider it pure joy, my brothers, when you face trials of many kinds, because you know that the testing of your faith develops perseverance. Perseverance must finish its work so that you may be mature and complete, not lacking anything." James 1:2-4

❧

"I will not die but live and will proclaim what the Lord has done." Psalm 118:17

❧

"I have told you these things, so that in me you may have peace. In this world you will have trouble. But take heart! I have overcome the world." John 16:33

❧

"But He said to me, "My grace is sufficient for you, for my power is made perfect in weakness." Therefore I will boast all the more gladly about my weaknesses, so that Christ's power may rest on me. That is why, for Christ's sake, I delight in weaknesses, in insults, in hardships, in persecutions, in difficulties. For when I am weak, then I am strong." 2 Corinthians 12:9-10

❦

"But He was pierced for our transgressions, He was crushed for our iniquities; the punishment that brought us peace was upon Him. And by His wounds we are healed." Isaiah 53:5

❦

"Know therefore that the Lord your God is God: He is the faithful God, keeping His covenant of love to a thousand generations of those who love Him and keep His commands." Deuteronomy 7:9

❧

"The Lord is close to the broken-hearted and saves those who are crushed in spirit." Psalm 34:18

❧

"Being confident of this, that He who began a good work in you will carry it on to completion until the day of Christ Jesus." Philippians 1:6

❧

"Have I not commanded you? Be strong and courageous. Do not be terrified; do not be discouraged, for the Lord your God will be with you wherever you go." Joshua 1:9

❧

"You dear children, are from God and have overcome them, because the One who is in you is greater than the one who is in the world." 1 John 4:4

"The Lord will fight for you; you need only to be still." Exodus 14:14

৫৩

"And we know that in all things God works for the good of those who love Him, who have been called according to His purpose." Romans 8:28

৫৩

"For God did not give us a spirit of timidity, but a spirit of power, of love and of self-discipline." 2 Timothy 1:7

৫৩

"Praise be to the God and Father of our Lord, Jesus Christ, the Father of compassion and the God of all comfort, who comforts us in all our troubles, so that we can comfort those in any trouble with the comfort we ourselves have received from God." 2 Corinthians 1:3-4

❧

"Find rest, O my soul, in God alone; my hope comes from Him." Psalm 21:22

❧

"And my God will meet all your needs according to His glorious riches in Christ Jesus." Philippians 4:19

❧

"Let the peace of Christ rule in your hearts, since as members of one body you were called to peace. And be thankful." Colossians 3:15

❧

"But seek first His kingdom and His righteousness and all these things will be given to you as well." Matthew 6:33

❧

"Therefore, my dear brothers, stand firm. Let nothing move you. Always give yourselves fully to the work of the Lord, because you know that your labor in the Lord is not in vain." 1 Corinthians 15:58

❧

"The sting of death is sin, and the power of sin is the law. But thanks be to God! He gives us the victory through our Lord Jesus Christ." 1 Corinthians 15:56-57

"Finally brothers, whatever is true, whatever is noble, whatever is right, whatever is pure, whatever is lovely, whatever is admirable—if anything is excellent or praiseworthy—think about such things." Philippians 4:8

❧

"I have learned the secret of being content in any and every situation, whether well fed or hungry, whether living in plenty or in want. I can do everything through Him who gives me strength." Philippians 4:12b-13

❧

"Therefore do not worry about tomorrow, for tomorrow will worry about itself. Each day has enough trouble of its own." Matthew 6:34

❧

"Look at the birds of the air; they do not sow or reap or store away in barns, and yet your Heavenly Father feeds them. Are you not more more valuable than they? Who of you by worrying can add a single hour to his life?" Matthew 6:26-27

Meet Carole Lewis

DIRECTOR EMERITUS OF FIRST PLACE FOR HEALTH AND AUTHOR

A warm, transparent and humorous communicator, Carole is a popular speaker at First Place for Health Wellness Weeks, seminars, and conferences around the country. She is also the author of fifteen popular books, including

- *First Place 4 Health*
- *Give God a Year*
- *Better Together*
- *Hope 4 You*
- *Live Life Right Here, Right Now*
- *A Thankful Heart.*

Carole was widowed in 2014 and lives in Houston, Texas and has three adult children (one deceased), eight grandchildren and eleven great-grandchildren.

Made in the USA
Monee, IL
01 March 2022